DREAMS, LOVE, AND MUSIC

Asiah "The Continent" Million

The Pen Station

www.facebook.com/TheContinentASIAH

www.twitter.com/AsiahMillion

www.twitter.com/ThePenStation

www.instagram.com/TheContinent

www.soundcloud.com/AsiahTheContinent

DREAMS, LOVE, AND MUSIC

DREAM YOUR LIFE, THEN LIVE YOUR DREAMS

ASIAH MILLION

authorHOUSE®

AuthorHouse™
1663 Liberty Drive
Bloomington, IN 47403
www.authorhouse.com
Phone: 1 (800) 839-8640

Cover Photo
MUA and Wardrobe Stylist: Andrea Dixon for GlamaGirlCosmetics.com
Accessories: Ayanna Dixon
Hair: Rosenie Bermingham
Graphic Designer: Belimage International Group

Back Photo
Dwight Keaton
Diamondmine Productions, LLC.

Published by AuthorHouse 06/18/2015

ISBN: 978-1-5049-1814-5 (sc)
ISBN: 978-1-5049-1813-8 (e)

Library of Congress Control Number: 2015909769

CONTENTS

To my children, my world: Taiwan and Oceann

Family is everything:

My mother: Beverley Pierre-Louis

My siblings: Reita, Audrey, Dennis, John, Evan, and Amena

Extended siblings: Ronel, Welby, and Rosenie Bermingham

My nieces and nephews: Quanneisha, Ashlee, John Jr., Justin, Jarrell, Jamel, Evan Jr., Nicolai, Emlyn, Asia, Korea, Sana'a, Alysha, and David

God-kids and extended family: Tyree and Sakai Hardy; Omar Todman Jr.; Tizje and Kahia Little; Jayla Habib; Brittney, Jeffrey Jr., and Jordan Atkins; Adia Hottenstein

In memory of my father, Philippe "Papa" Pierre-Louis, who lost his battle with pancreatic cancer on September 11, 2013

PREFACE

This book was written with the intention to exhibit different perspectives and choices, to enable the reader to get the best out of life. I kept it short and concise purposely for an easy read.

My goal is to encourage you to focus on creating the life you want in a world full of distractions. I feel compelled to share my experience because many of us stand so straddled between the past and the future we seek to build that we become disconcerted in the present.

I wrote this book because I want you to get a chance to know and understand me—not only as a recording artist, singer/songwriter, life coach, or author—but as a woman who was once a little girl that wanted to take her own life.

I've read in the papers that the US hits highest suicide rate in 25 years. To be your true self in a world full of judgment is a great accomplishment. If I can save lives by sharing the story of how I survived, then my mission is accomplished. Happiness is a dream that I'm sure we all share. It requires taking ownership of your life and taking control of *you*!

If there is any information, experience, advice, or quotation here that you can use, please do, and share. But if there's something that doesn't apply, then simply—let it fly.

Enjoy.

ABOUT THE AUTHOR

Multi-platinum, Grammy Award-nominated songwriter and Recording Artist, Asiah "The Continent" Million reveals how she managed to write one of Mary J. Blige's biggest records, "Family Affair," after being dropped from her record label for choosing to put her family over her career. Coming from a dysfunctional family, in search of an escape from her unfortunate life as a child, she realized love is what she needed as her foundation. Asiah made the decision a long time ago, to stay alive, after contemplating suicide. I have a purpose. Obtaining a record deal, Writing a hit record, getting married, having children, and dealing with a bad break-up were all a part of God's plan for me. I feel compelled to help others achieve happiness through dream therapy, love therapy and music therapy. These are the things that kept me alive. "Dreams, Love, and Music." I am not perfect, but I found happiness in my imperfections. Happiness is the highest level of success. I am not selling anyone dreams, I just like to help others find their purpose and live the best lives they possibly can.

CHAPTER 1

The Great Escape

Born on February 6, 1976, in Laurelton, Queens, New York, the fifth child of seven, living in a household of dysfunction at its best, would describe my unchosen lifestyle growing up. There were seven kids, three bedrooms, a basement that was always shared or rented to other family members, more cousins that my father adopted, a whole lot of different personalities to deal with, a dog, a cat, fish, birds, and even a monkey at one point!

My mom had a lot to deal with. She would have had eight of us; there was a girl who would've been two years older than me, but passed away in utero because the umbilical cord was wrapped around her neck. My mom had to go through labor and then deliver a deceased baby girl, so she later asked me to name my daughter what would've been my sister's name. So I added Melodee to my daughter's middle name out of respect for my mom. As I got older, my mother expressed the emotional pain and psychological damage she had suffered from that experience. But as a child, as far as I can remember, my mother was always stressed out.

My family was always at war. The only thing we all seemed to do well was fight. By the time I was born, there were already four siblings ahead of me. Attention was the main thing everyone seemed to fight for. Since I was the fifth child in line, I already knew that I would never get my own attention, so the only thing left for me to do was pay attention.

We often hear stories about females being molested, sexually abused, or raped. I've heard them from close friends and family. And as I look at reality shows, talk shows, and the news, I hear similar stories from celebrities and women I've always looked up to for inspiration. Many women are coming out with their stories! It's unfortunate that so many of us have such stories that affect us in so many different ways. My story, however, is just a little different.

My bigger brothers' intentions were to protect me from having stories like that, so for the most part they didn't even acknowledge the fact that I had a vagina. They treated me like I was their little brother, and they often left me with no other choice but to think like a boy. I went through a lot. Raised by the wolves, no holds barred! Being a kid wasn't easy for me. My brothers experienced a lot of pressure from their peers and were often beaten up by older guys when they were younger. So they didn't want me to experience what they had gone through—from anyone. In their minds, that was the way to make me stronger, to get me tough and ready for the world. But what they didn't realize was that I began to see them as the people they were so busy trying to protect me from—my worst enemies.

There were so many of us, my mom trusted that we were all taking care of each other. She would check in from time to time and ask if everything was okay, but my brothers had a way of making her feel secure that everything was fine, and would send her on her way—with my head under the pillow and their hands over my mouth. If I cried or showed any signs of distress, I'd get beaten up even worse, so I pretty much knew that I had to play it cool and act as if everything was all fun and games if I wanted less problems.

My father worked the overnight shifts at a hospital, so when he came home in the morning he would go straight to bed. It seemed as if he was too tired to even say hi. He was never really there to protect me. He slept during the day. Both of my parents had a lot on their plates. They always seemed too busy for me, so it became clear that if I needed help I was going to have to help myself.

My sisters were much older than I was, so they did their own thing with their friends when they could. My oldest sister knew how to keep to herself. She would go and read a book, or go to my grandmother's house to get away from the chaos, and I always secretly admired that. Because I was so young, and she wanted to be free, bringing me with her would've been like raining on her own parade. It always seemed like she was off the hook from the family beat-downs, or at least she knew how to dodge them when they came her way. But my other sister was always a part of the action. When she was around, she took me out, bought me stylish clothes, gave me great gifts, and did my hair just the way I loved it. I thought we were cool with each other, and sometimes I even considered her my best friend. She'd helped me out when I had to defend myself against my brothers. Yet, I had to defend myself against her too. We'd fight, but I had no idea what we were fighting about. I was always on defense with her and I hated feeling that way.

One day she and my brother were having a big argument. I had just gotten home from school and wanted some peace of mind, but that never seemed to be a friend of ours, and I always wondered why, so I would try to figure out how to make peace. I listened closely to see what the fight was about because I wanted to come up with a solution to the problem. My brother accused her of eating his cookies, and she said she hadn't. So I went into the kitchen to try to be the mediator. They were both so passionate about this fight and it bothered me to see how deep they were making it. I looked behind the table and found the cookies, three in a pack, still closed on the floor. I was so glad, because now the problem would finally have a solution, and we could adopt unity as another sibling.

I held the package up and showed them that I had found the cookies. They both saw me, but nothing changed. My brother said, "She probably pushed them back there on purpose!"

And she said to him, "You probably pushed them back there just so you could blame me!" And they kept arguing. The argument was just so pointless to me, and it didn't make any sense. I tried to break it up but finally realized that it would only be a waste of my time.

As I walked away, (eating the cookies!) I realized that they were both addicted to drama. They didn't want a solution. Each of them wanted to be the winner—as if whoever could better control the other would win. That's just one example of the many feuds I experienced with my family, from the outside looking in. Many other times, I wasn't on the outside looking in; I was on the inside trying to get out—and trying to figure out how I'd got in it in the first place.

After a while, the gifts my sister gave me and the good things she did for me felt like a trick, like cheese in a mousetrap—a way to control and trap me, to keep me where she wanted me. Whenever I wanted to go somewhere that was peaceful for me, or do something that would allow me to escape the drama, she would flip on me and find a way to pull me back in. Somehow the battle grew bigger, and things got worse between us.

It got to a point where I didn't want to be home. The streets were safer. I didn't want to partake in any of my family's affairs. I love my family, but the truth was—though sometimes we fought for attention, control, or for no reason at all—at times we actually had valid reasons to fight. Sometimes we didn't eat because there was never enough food. When there was food, we had to fight for it. It became so contentious that we had to put our names on our own food, but that didn't work; someone would still take it. There were far too many of us to find out who took it. The same thing happened with toilet paper: I was lucky if I found a roll of paper in the bathroom. If I did, I had to take it and hide it, otherwise someone else would. Actually, I was lucky if I could even use the bathroom, because my siblings were always scheming their way in first, and staying there forever on purpose just to make each other mad, so they could laugh. Anything of value had to be hidden. Money, jewelry, name-brand clothes, and shoes were always missing. Someone would steal them and sell them. Nobody ever really knew who it was because everyone always said, "It wasn't me!" I was always on defense at home. I became a monster. I didn't want to be that way, but sometimes you become what you're around, and that's how I had to be if I wanted to survive.

I never truly had the opportunity to be the little girl that I really was. I often found myself thinking thoughts far too deep and violent— thoughts that little girls shouldn't be thinking—such as how to defend myself against my own family. Guns were nothing new to me. I had been taught to use them since I was young. It's really bad when you have to consider using a gun on the ones who taught you how! Instead, I would go across the street to the park by the highway, sit on the swings, and watch the cars speeding by on the Belt Parkway. And then I would begin to think about running onto the highway to end my life. I didn't want to live. I felt there was no way my situation would change. I'd had these thoughts since I was about four years old, and at fourteen it still seemed that waiting till I turned eighteen to live my own life was too long. Committing suicide seemed like the easier thing to do than continuing to live at home. But before my emotions could take control, my thoughts would shift. I would begin to wonder, *How would everybody feel if I killed myself?* And, *How would my mother live after a death like that?* Being alone, thinking my own thoughts, and feeling my own feelings made the stress of everyone else's feelings and ways of thinking begin to subside. The thoughts of suicide and my unfortunate life shifted to dreaming about the life I desired. I only felt suicidal when I couldn't be myself, when I was forced to be the person everybody else wanted me to be. It actually felt like rape—everybody taking a piece of me without my consent and making me be this hard, cruel, angry fighter when really I was just a little girl with big dreams. I figured if I was going to die, I'd rather die fighting for the life I really wanted to live. My reality sucked, and I was ready to die. It was my dreams that kept me alive!

Once I started to envision the life I wanted to live, and to see myself as the person I wanted to be, I would just sit outside and dream. I pictured lots of lights, big beautiful buildings, a big stage, lots of people—and I was sharing my voice with them. I was telling a story, but the story had a melody. I was having a deep, passionate conversation and sharing my experiences with the world. I was emoting melodically!

You would've thought I was crazy if you had seen me singing in the park alone. *I* thought I was crazy, but it still felt better to dream about a good life than to think of committing suicide because of an unfortunate life. After coming from the park dreaming, I would run home to start preparing myself for that life. My family would think I had come home from jogging. They had no idea I was ready to opt out of life. I only jogged back home because I had a new perspective on things, and I was excited about life and living my dreams. It was that state of mind that made me focus on all of the good things about my family.

My father made us worship, sing church songs, and pray together every Friday night, which was the Sabbath. He made porridge Haitian style every Saturday morning before church. That brought us all to the table, together. It even brought all of the kids on the block of 238th Street to our house. My brother was a DJ. He often played music in the house super-loud. Even when my mother would yell and tell him to turn it down, he'd put on her favorite music and have her dancing in her misery.

Q-Tip and Phife from A Tribe Called Quest would come over after school to create music in the basement with my brother. They had no idea, but after my brother kicked me out of the basement, I would go upstairs and listen through the vents. They inspired me and didn't even know it. My oldest sister sang in the choirs at church, and would play the piano at home while I sang along. She is the one who set up my first solo in church when I was four years old. I sang "Jesus Loves Me" while she played the piano for me. My other sister gave me my first pink radio with a Whitney Houston cassette when I was in the fifth grade. That was one of the best gifts I ever received. She was creative and knew exactly how to choose the perfect gifts for everyone. That pink radio was the base of my homemade studio setup, and I would record myself singing just to see how I'd sound.

My other brother joined the army. Whenever he came home, he would wake us early in the morning and make us work out and clean the house thoroughly. He taught me how to discipline my mind regardless of what was going on around me. My younger brother and I would pretend we were television entertainers or superheroes. We would dress up in costumes and pretend to perform—acting, singing, and fighting. I was older then he was, so I finally had someone to boss around, but my first choice was to do artist development. Then, when my little sister came along, I'd make her sing and repeat after me. I showed her how to do vocal tricks and riffs before she could even talk.

Music is life to me. Music is what kept me alive. I would be punished and beaten up worse if I cried or showed emotions—because it showed weakness, in my brothers' minds. So I was able to live through music because it allowed me to express my feelings creatively, not negatively.

Once my family and close friends found out that I could sing, they didn't understand that it was my escape from death and my only way of life. My brother heard me one night by accident because I had fallen asleep listening to what I had recorded of myself on my pink radio. He woke me up at three in the morning and made me come downstairs and sing for his friends. I often felt as if they were pimping me. They made me sing just so they could get the *props*, or money. I didn't feel fully comfortable singing all the time if we weren't actually working toward something. I had a dream; I wanted to make plans, set goals, and then go after them. If we didn't discuss a bigger purpose than singing for its own sake, I'd question their intentions. They wanted me to sing for their own entertainment. But my thoughts were, *Do you understand that I'm not happy?* I didn't even want to be alive in those living conditions. I didn't want to sing just because I could and they wanted me to. I was ready to sing if they were just as willing to get out of the misery as I was and ready to make a better lifestyle out of it together. My mind wasn't only on the talent. It was on the whole movement and the work that was required to make it happen. I needed them to help me with my life. I wanted a team that would push me so that we could all benefit, but my singing seemed to be for their benefit only. Singing with no purpose was like trying to get me to talk about my feelings—not easy or fun to do, since I was routinely beaten up and taught to keep my feelings to myself. It was kind of private, and a very delicate, sensitive issue. So I shut down for the most part, if there wasn't a team with the same dream.

Regardless of our different personalities and the fights we had at home, we love each other and always have each other's back. We could be mad at each other one minute and cracking jokes, laughing out loud the next. It's hard for me to hold grudges, but easy to see when I deserve better. Instead of staying mad, I stayed busy. Instead of focusing on fighting my family, I'd dream about a better life, and that's what I wanted to fight for.

My parents didn't have enough money to put us in any activities. There were too many of us, and they were struggling just to feed us, so they balanced it out by keeping us in church and private school. Our church was our school and my mother was the secretary, so from Monday to Friday we went to school. Friday night was choir rehearsal and Saturday was our day of worship. Saturday nights were social events and basketball games against other Seventh-day Adventist churches. And Sunday was Pathfinders (something like a coed Girl and Boy Scouts), basketball and cheerleading practice. When we weren't home, we were at the church and private school—seven days a week.

When I was in the second grade, my mother let me go to the public school near my house with the neighborhood kids. I had the opportunity to exercise my talents because we had a dance club and talent shows that we spent a lot of our time practicing for. But my mother crushed my dreams without realizing it when she took me out of that school to put me back into private school. She said I was getting too worldly.

The choirs and groups that I sang with in church were what gave me life. My choir traveled, entered competitions, won a few times in the McDonald's Gospel Fest, and had our own yearly concerts, so these were the things that kept me hopeful. But I still had deep thoughts and bad feelings while at church. I couldn't envision my dreams or my purpose going to church with a bunch of church people who were very judgmental and controlling. I believed in God, but the religion just seemed like a bunch of people who wanted to play follow-the-leader. They had the power to kick people out of church, a practice known as *dis-fellowship*. The church was pretty strict. I found myself, again, not able to be myself, and I was always on defense. I don't remember many people talking to me to see what was going on in my life or trying to help. There were only a few. Instead, I felt looked upon with judgment and hate.

Growing up, we couldn't pierce our ears or wear jewelry, nail polish, or makeup. So, basically—no creativity! No television or any form of activities outside of religion from sundown Friday to sundown Saturday. This was called the Sabbath. We had to keep the Sabbath holy, which is in the Bible, but I always had questions about the manmade rules that were never thoroughly answered. Every time I went to church, it seemed as if they added a new rule. No curling your hair on the Sabbath, no cooking, no nothing! I was scared to breathe. I was accused of "looking like I was at a club" while singing in church once, because I was feeling the music. They seemed to focus more on minding everyone else's business than praising God, which is what robbed me of being able to let loose emotionally, spiritually, and musically.

I'm thankful that my parents made me go to church; again, I took the good and ran with it, but the bad was really bad for me. The religion and the ways of church folk had me build a brick wall around myself. It was the music that allowed me to put my guard down and connect, but since they criticized the way I enjoyed the music, I didn't want to have anything to do with the church. It was God that I wanted everything to do with. I could feel the presence of God when I was alone more than when I was at my church. So I decided to pursue my relationship with God—not the church.

Finally, I made it to high school—Andrew Jackson High in Queens— where I was able to develop a better sense of self. It seemed like a whole new world to me. Everyone was free to be themselves. Style, jewelry, swagger, and the latest fashions were a big deal for me. I liked to dress in a way that allowed me to feel free, and I had been denied that privilege for far too long where I came from. I had to wear a school uniform during all of my private school years.

The first class I signed up for was gospel chorus. That seemed more important to me than school itself. The day I realized music saved my life was the day I planned to live every day preparing myself to be ready for the opportunity, whenever I'd find it. I never really knew exactly what or when it would be, but living it and preparing for it is what brought me comfort. Generally, I'm happy because of my natural high for music and life. The only thing that someone could really do to set me on fire was to distract and pull me away from the one thing I looked forward to every day.

To this day, my little brother owes me Karen White and Run DMC cassettes because he popped my tapes when we were younger just to get me mad. That was the only way he could gain my attention or win when we had our little tiffs.

In high school, students fought; females were walking around pregnant; people cut school to go outside and smoke. It was so refreshing to see everyone being themselves. Not that it was right, but everyone has problems and everyone deals with them differently. It showed me how many other people were coming from broken homes and that I wasn't alone. It made me feel I could be myself, no hiding. When the bad was at its worst, it was the music that kept me at my best and brought balance. We'd spend a lot of our days preparing for the concerts. My experience with the school choir was different from church because although we were singing gospel music, everyone was able to be themselves. We all had issues at home, but regardless of our problems, everyone came ready to sing praises to the Lord, in harmony, wearing makeup, jewelry, hair dye, and stylish clothes, and being whomever we wanted to be, with no judgment.

My only problem was that I still didn't feel I was being myself. Yes, I loved God, and I loved singing gospel music, but I wanted to be more relatable to people. I was a little girl who had a crush on boys and wanted to explore relationships. I loved fashion and had started to learn how to cut, braid, and dye hair and experiment with my creative side. Those were the things I wanted to sing about—real things that real people go through. I wanted to be truthful and honest. So many girls had babies or were pregnant. I saw everyone swap boyfriends and girlfriends in school and make a big deal out of going to the senior prom. I didn't want to be a part of any of that, but that's what I wanted to sing about. When church people lie down together in bed with their husbands or wives, I'm pretty sure they don't want to hear gospel music. They need music to get them in the mood. God made sex. It's a beautiful thing when done properly. I like to create music to support love and relationships.

In the lunchroom, *freestyling* at the table had become our favorite thing to do. It brought a big crowd of creative people together. One day, Fame Fortune took his position and started making beats on the table,

I started singing, and rappers from all over the lunchroom came to our table to join in. That's what brought us together and was our way of getting to know each other. After I left the table and was on my way to my next class, Ma Barker, a female rapper, approached me and complimented me on my voice. She wanted to introduce me to two other females that could sing because she was trying to put a girl group together. That is exactly what I was looking for. We talked a little about ideas. She had written a song for them already and she just needed another female to add to the group.

I met the girls and we clicked the moment we heard each other sing. There's something about music that connects me to people. I had seen these girls my whole freshman year. One of them would look at me and keep walking like she owned the hallways. We never said a word to each other. The other one was in my homeroom class. She was always smiling and making friends with everyone, but I didn't know either one of them could sing. The moment we sang for each other, it was as if we all fell in love. A creative love! We practiced in the basement of Ma Barker's mother's hair shop on Farmers Boulevard once in a while, but she was so focused on her own rap career that she left us to do our own thing. We connected from time to time, but it was weird how we understood each other. It was always love and respect whenever we did see each other. Ma Barker was running her own race, so it was as if she handed me the baton, and I took it from there and ran with it.

I suggested that we be consistent and set at least one day out of the week to practice, so Erin volunteered her house. Every Wednesday, Southside Jamaica, Queens, became our place to be. Of course, on the way there, boys in nice cars would stop to talk to us and we'd flirt a little bit, exchange numbers, and maybe go out just for fun. But for the most part, we were serious about our rehearsals. We had to walk a few long blocks after getting off the bus before we got to Erin's house, so sometimes— especially in the cold—we appreciated the rides from guys. We were always meeting new people that would introduce us to someone that knew someone else that had a cousin or a brother that could help us out with our music. One day, we met a producer who really liked us, and when he saw that we practiced on our own consistently, he believed in us and helped us out.

The first time we had a meeting in the city was when it all became real to me. We had car service, the meeting was at the office of a major record company, and we felt like superstars. I felt my dreams were right at my fingertips. Reachable! Everything I had envisioned was there before my eyes. The lights from the city, the tall buildings, the energy—it was so exciting. We were in the city of New York, where dreams come true! As I turned to look at the other girls, I caught Erin's eyes. I saw the passion in hers and she saw it in mine. And then she said, "Wait, why do we look like tourists right now?" and we both laughed. We lived in Queens, only about twenty minutes away—so close, yet so far. We could go to the city anytime, but we didn't. It was exciting to be there that day. We weren't there to sightsee or shop. We were there to make our dreams come true.

This meeting was just to introduce us to the *artist and repertoire* (A&R) person. We didn't have music for them to hear. We'd never even been in the studio together. They just wanted to meet us and hear us sing. They loved what they heard and put us in contact with industry professionals that could give us the sound they were looking for.

Angie Stone was one of the first professional songwriters that we had the opportunity to meet and work with. We met a few times, she made us feel comfortable, shared high school stories with us, got a chance to know what we liked, and wrote a song that we all fell in love with. She knows what she wants to hear in her songs and took nothing less. I was used to that. My choir director was the same way when it came down to knowing our sectional notes (soprano, alto, tenor). That's another great experience that I appreciate from church. The vocal training stuck with me and prepared me for times and opportunities like these.

We had a very tense recording session. Recording vocals and trying to get the exact sound that you're looking for isn't always easy. This was our first time recording as a group with each other. We got a chance to see different sides of each other. After a few stressful moments, Angie decided it was best for us to go home and get some rest. We ended the session before the song was complete. Our producer told us he'd call us and let us know the next move.

The next day he called me and told me that Erin and I had done a good job, but the other group member was pitchy and needed a lot of work. He was frustrated and ready to give up. I told him we were going to work harder and that we were willing to do whatever we had to in order to develop ourselves and grow as a group. A week later, he brought us to a vocal coach in Brooklyn named Carine, whom, ironically, I had already known from church and mutual cousins. The first day with our vocal coach was our last day. That's when everything changed. She showed us some helpful vocal exercises, and then had us all sing individually. Pitch problems, uncontrollable vibratos, nervousness, and all kinds of vocal issues came to the surface. After that day, we never even heard back from that producer. The practices weren't as consistent. The studio session and the vocal session put a little pressure on us and showed us how much work it took.

I remember being home in the chaotic world of my family, praying, asking God, "Now, what?" I couldn't speak for anyone else, but for me, with all I was going through in my personal life, I needed this badly. I would call the girls to vent and talk about how we should keep going. Sometimes, they made me feel like I was crazy, and like I was an alien with seven heads and six lips But other times, I could feel their passion and willingness to keep going.

Where we came from, there were a lot of deep-rooted issues. Insecurities hold so many people back, causing them to focus on all the reasons why they *can't*. I saw things differently and spent much of my time trying to convince everyone that we *can*. I thought about all of the issues we had as black females growing up in the 'hood. The houses seem stuck together or built on top of each other, and everyone's living so close, more people than land, no personal space, and not many opportunities. So it's easy to step on each other's toes and fight. I'm from New York. Everyone's always so angry, aggressive, or defensive. I wanted to find a way out by embracing our differences and showing the world how talented we were, so I came up with the idea of adding another female and renaming the group from *Legacy* to *4 Shades of Black*. Light-skinned girls were favored and highly noticed, but were often accused of being conceited or stuck up. Dark-skinned girls were overlooked, made to feel useless and not good enough. Everyone had been conditioned to believe these things about themselves, but I saw the beauty in our culture. When I told them my idea, they saw the vision and got excited all over again. So we started looking for a fourth member. Each of us described ourselves by our complexion to fit our role in the group. Erin was the light-skinned one, I was the light brown one, China was the dark brown one, and all we needed was the dark-skinned member.

My time in high school was spent trying to make this group work. A few days later, Erin came to me and said she knew of someone that was dark-skinned, beautiful, and had vocals that were on point. Erin introduced us, but we were also familiar with each other from gospel chorus. We'd never exchanged words, but she had a beautiful voice. From that moment on, we spent a lot of time together, practicing, taking pictures, and sharing ideas, until one day we received bad news. Erin's parents had decided to move to Alabama, which meant Erin had to go also. That was so crazy to me. It felt as if someone had thrown a dart right in the middle of my dreams. Every time something good happened, something contrary would also happen. Erin and I were the two consistent ones. We sang "Sweet Thing" at our high school talent show together because we couldn't get ahold of the other members. We came in second place, but we were furious because we wanted first place. We were inspired to go harder after that talent show. We had a callback to audition for *Sister Act 2*, but since Erin found out she had to move, I didn't have the urge to go. It didn't feel the same going alone. I guess I was just focused on keeping a group together. I was so used to the bond, the collaboration, and the unity in our group.

The day before Erin moved, we all went to her house, hugged, kissed, cried, and said our good-byes. We had just found the fourth dark-skinned singer, and now we had to replace the light-skinned one. Erin told me to keep going and that she'd be supportive from wherever she was. To have that support from her even though she couldn't be a part of it gave me the confidence I needed to keep going. Although I knew I'd miss her, I still considered her part of the team.

Back to school auditioning! Everyone that knew me knew I was always singing and looking for other singers as well. I had many different ideas. My focus was to have an official group before graduation, but the challenge was finding others who were just as focused. My friend Joanne would often sing to me, in an operatic, high, playful tone in the hallways. She had a great voice and was into the arts but more into fashion, style, and cosmetology. My high school wasn't a school of the arts, so of course, not many people understood me. Most thought I was crazy because all I wanted to do was sing and dream. So whenever I came across other creative students, we clicked, stuck together, pushed, and supported each other. Joanne is one of the few who understood me and was always helpful and supportive. She told someone who knew someone else that introduced me to a light-skinned female singer named Janai. The moment I heard Janai sing I was blown away. No pitch problems or nervousness, and her riffs were on point. I couldn't wait to introduce her to the other girls of 4 Shades of Black.

Every time I called the girls, Janai was the only one available. Two weeks after graduation, I received a call from Big Baby— who played the piano in gospel chorus. He called to tell me that he and his partner, Suga Mike, had a connection with a major record company. He said if we were ready to work hard, he could get us a deal. I didn't have an official group, but I told him I'd call him right back. I got off the phone with Big Baby and called every single one of my female friends that could sing. Janai was the only one responsive. I called Big Baby and told him that I didn't quite have a full group, but the one I had was really good. So the plan was for Janai and me to start recording songs and then add the other two girls later on.

Once we got in the studio, we really didn't want to be anywhere else. We were young and surrounded by lots of friends. We loved to do fun things, but no matter where we were, even if we were just hanging out or partying, we always had the mind-set of *you never know who you're going to meet.* So we carried ourselves as if someone were always watching, and we always wanted to be ready.

One day, I happened to be in the right place at the right time. I worked at JCPenney in Green Acres mall. I tried to stay as low key as possible because I didn't really want anyone to know that I worked there. In my mind, I was going to have a record deal. I only needed the money from my job so I could get around, buy nice clothes, and invest in myself. It worked out perfectly when I was placed in the basement working in the girls' department. No one in the mall could see me except parents with young kids who came downstairs inside the store.

One day, my manager sent me to work upstairs at the front mall entrance to get customers to sign up for a JCPenney credit card. "Why me?" I asked. That was exactly where I did not want to be.

She said, "Because I like the way you deal with people. I see how they take to you. You'll get a dollar in cash plus your regular paycheck for everyone you sign up."

Upstairs at the front door, I had just finished signing a lady up for a charge card. As soon as she walked away from me, I saw her hug this guy and stand there for about ten minutes talking to him. I couldn't see his face because his back was facing me. Once they were done talking, he turned around and I realized it was LL Cool J. He walked over to my table and started to look at the applications to see what was going on, so I said, "Hi, would you like to apply for a JCPenney charge card?"

He looked at me like, *Seriously?* Then he laughed and said, "No, but if there's any way I could support, let me know." So I asked him if he'd mind listening to some of the music that I had been recently working on.

At first he was hesitant, but then he asked what type of music it was. He asked if I was an aspiring rapper, but once I told him that I could sing, he looked excited. He gave me his beeper number and told me that he needed a female vocalist for music he was currently working on. A few days later on my day off, I beeped him and he called back, surprisingly. He came to pick me up from my house in his red Porsche. He introduced himself to my mother, and then took me to his record company, Uncle L's, which was on Hillside Avenue in Queens. He played me some of his music and listened to mine. He introduced me to the staff, and a studio session was set up for me to record vocals.

Being in the studio with LL Cool J, listening to a song come alive with *my* vocals on *his* record—someone who had bona fide, consistent hits—made me forget about my reality. It was now eleven in the morning, and

I had just remembered that I was supposed to be at work—at Green Acres Mall in Long Island—to open at ten. I was still in Manhattan, at the studio where the session had started at nine the night before. After I laid my vocals down, I sat there and watched him work consistently until he got the record the way he wanted it. To be a part of that process changed my whole life. I never even saw JCPenney a day after that. I took that energy and walked by faith toward the direction of my dreams.

I spent my days and nights working on more songs with Janai, Big Baby, and Suga Mike. One year after graduating high school, we were standing in front of record executives that were ready to sign us immediately. We still didn't have the other two females, but they liked the idea of just the two of us. "Two seventeen-year-old, around-the-way girls" were the words used to describe us after we shared our vision. We all agreed, shook hands, and we got the deal. We went from *4 Shades of Black* to a duo called *Sa-Deuce*, meaning *the two. It's a deuce!*

A record deal—how crazy was that! I never thought that it was going to happen. I knew I'd planned to die trying, but I honestly thought that I'd die before it happened. Where I came from, opportunities like this didn't come around every day. They didn't come around at all, actually. Trouble came our way constantly, the ice cream truck came every night in the summertime, boys came our way from everywhere in the world; even Akim came all the way to Queens from Africa to find his bride in the film *Coming To America*. People came and went, parties happened all the time, girl scouts and Jehovah's Witnesses came knocking at our doors—but dreams and opportunities like this one *never* came knocking on our doors. So we hopped on that opportunity as though it was the last time we'd ever see one.

Traveling to different states, performing on various stages, seeing new places, meeting new faces, doing promotional tours, giving radio interviews ... long days, short nights, studio, gym, sacrifices, eating healthy, artist development—and getting paid to do all these things! It was a dream come true. All our hard work had paid off.

Our schedule was set, and mandatory, just like school. Every day we had to be in the gym at one. We'd stay until about four, then we had two hours to eat and get to the studio. Our sessions were from six in the evening to six in the morning every day for two months, because we had an album release date.

After completing the album, our first trip out of town was to Virginia Beach, Virginia. I can't remember the next trip. It picked up so quickly, and we were traveling every week for days, weeks, and sometimes months at a time. We recorded our first single and put out our first video, "Don't Waste My Time." Everything was moving smoothly. We were highly excited.

It wasn't until it came time to choose our second single that things started to change. The Record Company Executives chose "Body Knocking." The treatment was totally different from the first video. Before we signed the agreement, they told us they loved our style. We were two *around-the-way* girls representing all the girls that wanted to make it out of the 'hood. We were the kind of girls that were comfortable enough in our femininity to wear timberland boots and sneakers. We were confident intellectually, and wanted to be role models for the girls who wanted more out of life than just to remain in the ghetto neighborhoods that they were born in. We wanted to be an inspiration and wear stylish clothes, to promote the idea that we didn't have to take our clothes off and be sexual to look good. We had a vision and a plan. The record company loved it and agreed.

Once we hit the gym and started training hard, our stylist started to bring us clothes that looked as though they could have been designed for Adina Howard. She was our label mate, and her stylist was our stylist, who had later become our manager. I requested to use a different song, such as "One-Man Woman," which promoted nurturing relationships and not just occasional, purposeless sex with random guys. When the record company decided to go with "Body Knocking" instead, it made me feel as though we didn't matter.

They were marketing us as two seventeen-year-old girls, but they had us singing songs like "Go Down" and "Body Knocking." Our age and the song choices didn't go together. Those songs were far too mature for what we wanted to promote, but we were told to write them anyway, and to reference them as if they were for Adina Howard. Clearly, that was just trickery, because they ended up on our album and one of them became our second single. I think they're great records. We wrote them, but not for ourselves. It was that type of thing that made me feel less excited. They were trying to give us a particular image, but we were who we were. I was proud of the standards I had set for myself.

We even argued over the pictures from the photo shoots. I'm very playful and silly when I get tired. After a long day of shooting and taking professional pictures, I would stick my tongue out and have fun. That's what would keep me going when I was ready to wrap up the shoot and go home to get some rest but couldn't because it wasn't over. I thought they knew I was just joking around and that those pictures would be kept private. But out of all of the beautiful pictures, they chose the ones of me with my tongue out or of us being sexy in a silly way. I learned from my mistakes, and now I'm more mindful of what I do on camera and in public. But even behind the scenes, they changed the plan. The game changed, the whole purpose changed, and I started to lose myself. I vented to my manager about how I was feeling, but she saw everything from the record company's point of view and tried to persuade me to go with the flow. I began to talk less and listen more. Instead of basking in the attention that I was receiving as an artist to excite me, and blind me, it served me better to be the one to *pay* attention. I had mastered the art of paying attention many years ago. I got the confirmation that she was a part of the record company's team, not ours.

Management was supposed to protect us as artists from the record company's shenanigans. But everything after that was a big battle—war at home and war at work too. I didn't know what to do or whom to call, so I called God. I began to spend more time praying. Again, the feeling of being forced to be someone I wasn't became a huge issue in my life. The manipulative actions, harsh words, and malicious ways all made me feel as if I was being un-agreeably screwed in the rear end, with no grease. That hurts!

It began to be clear that the deal I'd entered into wasn't the best for me. But I had already signed the contract, so quitting wasn't an option. I was ready to do what I had to do to keep moving forward. Ironically, a few days before our second video shoot, I found out that I was pregnant. I had prayed for a way out, but it hadn't hit me that this was it. I was more inspired to continue working because now I was going to have a baby to take care of. Although I experienced a bad case of morning sickness and threw up all day, I still put on what the stylist gave me and played the part. I didn't like the way they styled us for this second video. It was totally different from the first one. I felt very uncomfortable because "Body Knocking" was not what we wanted to promote. However, I didn't complain much; I expressed myself a few times but didn't let my feelings dictate my work performance. I was happy to be working. Months later, I was still working. I was four months pregnant when we went to L.A. to perform on *Soul Train*. My manager styled us and specifically chose a bigger jacket for me to cover my belly. I thought everything was cool, so I was hurt when I found out that the record company didn't support my pregnancy. I was ready to work until the last minute. I would only be pregnant for nine months, and I had already worked for four of them. I didn't want to go home; I wanted to go harder! This was one of the real things that real people go through—the life of a female. I wanted to inspire others who had become pregnant to keep going.

Nevertheless, I had to make a decision: Would I keep my baby and lose my deal, or have an abortion and keep the deal? As I weighed my options, I realized that *love* was the missing element in my home that had made me go so hard for my music career. Now that I had the opportunity to give love a try and start my own family, I knew that was what I needed as my foundation.

Max Gousse, the CEO who had signed me, somehow made me feel that he still believed in me. He told me I was very talented and way ahead of my time. I understood that they had to do what they felt was best for the company. But at the same time, I had to do what I felt was best for me.

Gracefully moving forward, I chose to start my family. I prayed constantly and kept God first. I got the answers I was looking for. With

God on my side, I was confident enough to step out on faith, believe in myself, take the longer route, and create the type of business that worked better with my beliefs.

I followed my heart and embraced the new life living within me. Music had always been a great escape, but now I had a chance to experience another dream of mine—love! I had never really had love or any other reason to live before my record deal. My family loved me in their own way, but I never had the chance to *feel* what love was supposed to feel like. Now was my chance to create my own family—the kind of family I wished I'd had.

Getting a record deal with the backing of a major company was one of the best opportunities I've experienced. I'm so thankful to everyone who believed in me and made that possible. It was my first chance of proof that dreams do come true. It didn't make me a millionaire or a superstar, and because of that, people considered it a failure. But what some would consider a stumbling block was a stepping stone for me. This was an amazing chance of a lifetime to step up and begin the journey of finding my purpose and becoming the woman I am today— and am still becoming.

CHAPTER 2

Love and Music

Back to the basics- in the chaotic world of my home, again I found myself asking God, "Now, what?" But this time was different. I had just traveled around part of the world. I'd seen a lot and grown so much. I thanked God for that experience. I viewed my music associates as family. I didn't want to let that go. *Should I fight for the label and try to convince them to support me? Or should I just trust that God has something else in store for me if I move forward?* I definitely had something to look forward to. I had "love" growing inside of me. And I didn't have a one-night stand; I had a man who was supportive of my music career, who could relate because he was focused on his own music career. This was someone who had become my friend, whom I could vent to, who could vent to me, who was equally ready to own our new situation and start a family together.

While I was pregnant and at home waiting to give birth to my son, I couldn't stop thinking about the kind of life I wanted him to have. I knew I didn't want him to live the kind of life I'd had growing up, and since I had been blessed with the opportunity to travel and explore different ways of living, I couldn't stop dreaming. My dreams only got bigger. I wanted a better way for him. The more I felt my baby move, kick, and grow inside of me, the more I wanted to pursue my music career, but for a different reason. I no longer needed an escape. Now, I actually had something to live for.

Throughout my pregnancy I was more emotional than normal, and I needed to make sure that I stayed creative while expressing my emotions. I'd rather write songs and record them than talk to people because many times people rewrite your story. They rearrange the lyrics and it's no longer a musical. It becomes life drama. Creative writing was also my man's way of expressing himself. He was very quiet and usually avoided saying the wrong things, but when he did express himself, he would write. He was a recording artist signed to TVT Records with a publishing deal. He's from Queens as well, so we had a lot in common because we were both trying to come up—from living in Queens to living our dreams. We didn't have to speak constantly. Certain songs allowed us to silently enjoy each other's company. We shared the same kind of love for music. Music connected us—not the music industry but the music our hearts made when they beat together as one.

The moment I held my son in my arms, I checked his fingers, checked his toes, kissed him, and stared some more. Love had taken over me and then I started dreaming again. I wanted so much for him, and he deserved a better life than the one I had known. One of the things that kept my relationship with my man going was that I didn't lose myself, and I supported him not losing himself as well. I started going to the gym immediately after my six-week checkup. I communicated with a lot of the producers, singers, songwriters, and industry associates that I had met throughout my journey. Having a baby did not mean my dreams were over or that my whole life was *baby, baby, baby.*

I went to the studio as often as I could. I did vocal coaching and reference work to keep extra money in my pocket while patiently waiting and working on the next big thing.

One thing I always did was keep my relationship consistent with God. I always prayed to God with one of the most sincere questions: "Now what, God?" And I was always appreciative for the things I received. I thanked God constantly, no matter what situation I was in. But in the meantime and the in-between time, my question to God was, "What do you want me to do with my life?"

I thought about working on a solo album, but at the same time I was open to experimenting and trying new things. Going solo wasn't really my thing because I was so used to singing in harmony. I loved the togetherness and the different elements that groups brought together. I was still in contact with many of the female singers that I had met in school, and my best friend from church who sang in the choir with me—who's also an amazing writer. So I figured, with all these creative people around me, why not explore? Ironically, my best friend's son and mine were born five days apart. There's nothing like supporting each other and accomplishing goals together, so I was open to the many different possibilities.

I was already living proof that dreams do come true. Quitting wasn't an option. My mind was already opened and my heart was already in it. Traveling and getting paid to do what I loved had brought me to another level of consciousness. The way we moved in the 'hood was so different from the way other cultures moved. I was not content accepting what society had given to us. I wanted more out of life. Society had beaten me up. My family had beaten me up. The music industry had beaten me up. My friends were all I had. I'd seen the ways that high-end celebrities lived and how they were getting the better things in life, so I took note. I felt we deserved that way of living also. Society had stuck us all together in a small ghetto neighborhood with nothing to look forward to, but there was a whole world out there. We didn't have to settle and accept what was given to us. I knew that if we put the work in together, we could make it together.

My relationship with my son's father was pretty simple because, for one, I wasn't needy. I didn't require much attention because from my youth I had already mastered the art of *paying* attention. I never got the kind of attention I needed, so it made me feel good to be the one to give the attention. I didn't expect it from my own family, so the attention my man did give me was always enough and appreciated. We slept in the same bed every night, had some phenomenal sex that put each other to bed, and woke each other up in the morning. That was enough gas in my tank for me to ride the waves of life. Plus, I had my friends for those days when we just needed to vent, talk about feelings, eat lots of food, support each other, and not have to worry about any of life's turbulence.

We would sit around and cry and talk about ways to make money. After the movie *Set It Off* came out, we even entertained ourselves and talked about ways to rob a bank. Although we knew we weren't going to rob a bank, it was still fun to dream about getting all of that money together. It was so real for us. Since we all sang and wrote, we spent a lot of time creating and sharing ideas.

I think my ability to balance working on my music and goals with being a mother and developing my relationship is one of the things that kept my son's father attracted to me. I didn't depend on him or pressure him for anything. As long as I had a vision, my energy was on a million, and he was happy because I was happy. He hated it when I wasn't happy, so he supported me pursuing my dreams and spending time with friends. He did have an issue with the fact that I didn't cook as often as he would've liked. But he saw the bigger picture once he realized how passionate I was about my dreams. The friendship was good, the sex was great, and I happened to get pregnant and have his baby. But that still didn't make me his wife. He hadn't put a ring on my finger, and I never lost sight of that. I wasn't putting his needs before mine. Those were my rules, and I was fine with no ring—because I had goals of my own and was focused. I was happy with the way things were. I could tell he wanted me to put him first and do more for him, but he played it cool. He knew he hadn't gained enough points for that yet. His mother allowed me and our son to stay with them, but that was temporary. I was thankful, but it wasn't my own. To me, I was homeless. He hadn't provided a place of our own for me to cook in, so that is what I focused on.

One night I was getting dressed to go out with my girlfriends. He looked at me and told me to change my clothes. He said he didn't want me showing everybody "his" body. It was summertime, and I looked cute, but I wasn't showing the goodies. However, it still bothered him. I gave him a sweet hug and explained to him that it was my body and not his. I showed him my finger so he could see that I didn't have a ring on it. I told him that it was ladies' night out, and that I was only going to be with my girls. Thursday nights and some Tuesdays were our nights out, since we all had family and other obligations. I told him not to worry and that I'd get nice and toasty and come home to him, and those nights were always super-amazing for us. He knew if I came home happy, he'd wake up happier. Weeks later, I got a ring. From that moment on, things changed. If I was going to be a wife, I needed to be a good one. I had to get serious about my life and get another accomplishment.

I found myself asking again, "Now what, God?" Every night and day I was praying, working, dreaming, and thinking of a master plan. All my friends had day jobs. Me? All I had was a daydream. I had been dropped from my record label in 1996. It was now 2001, and I didn't have a deal. My son was starting to become aware. I couldn't do as much for him as I wanted to. We were living in my man's parents' house. I was a grown woman. I needed my own space. I'd worked on so many different projects with so many different producers and went through a few management companies. I revisited the 4 Shades of Black project with my friends. That didn't work out. Our levels of focus and passion differed. We fought more then we worked, so because of my love for them, I decided I'd rather just stay friends than force something that didn't fit and try to convince them to be professional R & B singers. My days had me wondering, *What am I going to do with my life?* I was getting married. That was major. Who doesn't dream of *love*? I was excited, but at the same time, I wasn't quite ready. If I was going to give my life to someone, I needed to have something to bring—not only to the table, but into a house—the home that we would call our own.

Furious, on my knees one night I prayed to God. I prayed so hard and long that I fell asleep crying and praying. I knew I must've fallen asleep because I was awakened with one of the craziest dreams ever. It was so clear and confirmed so much for me. It answered the question that I'd been praying about for years: *Why am I not accomplishing anything?* I was sweating profusely. In the dream, I was outside on a big track running a race. I saw my entire family at the finish line cheering me on. My mother's face stood out, but all of my siblings and many others were there as well. My childhood best friend Tracey was there; my high school friend and partner Erin was there; my partner of Sa-Deuce and friend Janai was there, screaming for me to win. It was crazy because I hadn't even spoken to any of them for a while. When I turned around, I saw a few people at the starting line, mad at me for being "on track", running. I started crying when I noticed that the main person trying to hold me back was one of my closest friends. She was yelling at me, trying to grab my hand, telling me not to go. I turned back around and saw my family—the people who I had thought were my worst enemies—cheering me on, yelling my name, and pushing me to win. I was kind of confused. Were they enemies, or did I just have some heavy-duty training? That was a perfect example of one of the things that made me stronger since it didn't kill me. I used what they had taught me and shook off everything that was holding me back. I ran with everything I had until I hit the finish line.

Focus was the answer to my prayers. I wasn't as focused as I needed to be in order to make things happen. In my dream, it was made clear that I had to stop living the way others wanted me to live and be who I was. Focus on myself, my goals, my dreams, my family, my purpose, my future. Not my problems, my setbacks, my failures, my past, my friends and their problems. Many of the people that were close to me developed feelings because my focus took away from what they wanted from me. But God had answered my prayers. I was so connected to God that I wasn't concerned about who I was offending anymore. I trusted that God would work things out. I was finally back on track, so I stayed *in my lane* and focused on winning. I was unstoppable, fearless, and nonnegotiable because my family needed me. My son saw me writing at home constantly, leaving to go to work in the studio, and not coming home for long periods of time. But he never saw anything to show for it. His father saw me coming home late at night—or sometimes not at all—but rarely saw me in the kitchen cooking. My son needed his mother, and his father needed me to be his wife. And I wanted to make that happen.

Weeks later, I received a phone call from Mary J. Blige's management saying she had heard the record we did with her brother and loved it. "*Wow*, look at God!" When you pray to God for something, pay attention to the answers, even if they scare you. God had placed the right people in my life at the right time. He knew what he was doing. One of the people who made this possible was Lelee, from the group SWV. Every time she came to New York, she would call me. I had met Lelee years prior, before I even had a record deal. We met through

27

another young lady who believed in me and wanted to manage me. This woman was one of the *baddest* females I've ever met—not only because she was beautiful and had a body to die for but because she had a heart of gold. Her name was Natalie. She arranged for me to meet Lelee, so I brought Janai along. This was when SWV was at their peak. Lelee was super-busy, but communicated through Natalie, who was more hands-on with us.

One day, while Janai and I were in the studio, I received a disturbing phone call from Natalie's other partner, Errol. He told me that Natalie had been hit and killed by a drunk cop on Merrick Boulevard. I hit the floor! I was hurt badly for months. 226th Street in Laurelton, Queens, New York, was named after her: *Natalie Crossman Place*. Unfortunately, that is what brought Lelee and I closer.

One day, Lelee called me. She was in New York working out of LL Cool J's studio in Queens with a producer named Kiyamma. She introduced me to him, and said he was really talented and that I should come work there as often as possible. He had a week lock-in session, and it was only seven minutes from where I lived in Queens. I called my friends who were in the group 4 Shades of Black to come meet him and Lelee to try and get some work done as well. Being in a group with them hadn't worked out, but they were still my friends. I definitely wanted to see everyone succeed, whether it was with me, together, or apart. Kiyamma had come from the church and was big on gospel music, so I introduced him to the "dark-skinned" singer/songwriter from our group who had a big interest in gospel music. I also introduced him to my best friend—who I had suggested join the group as the "light-skinned" female, because her writing skills were phenomenal—and then to China, one of the original female singers that I had met in high school. China was the one that had a challenging time in the studio when we worked with Angie Stone and also was unavailable when I called her right before Janai and I got the record deal. This time around, she was more prepared. She did everything she could to perfect her craft. She asked me to give her vocal lessons and we worked out almost every day. She also bought studio equipment and went to school to study audio engineering just so we could continue to work and make it together. She even bought books on the music business, and when I had questions pertaining to law, agreements, and contracts she was able to explain a lot of the business to me.

Even though music had been my escape from my youth, I had some very creative friends around me, and we all had our personal issues. There's nothing like trying to make it with your friends. Teamwork always made the dream work! I told them all to feel free to call Kiyamma and develop their own relationships so that they could work on their own time. I was signed to Nathan of Gaman Entertainment Management Company. He had me working out of Sean "Diddy" Combs' studio, *Daddy's House*, constantly, so I couldn't be there as much as I wanted to be. There were always various songwriters, singers, and producers coming in and out, working as much as they could. Whenever I did have the opportunity to go to their studio, China was always there working already.

One day at the studio, China and I wrote a song with Brucie, a songwriter who was working on a remix for his sister Mary. J. Blige's *No More Drama* album. I called my best friend to invite her to come to the studio, but it was her mother's birthday and they were going out to dinner. I remember being on the phone with her, venting. I was having one of those days where I was so tired of constantly working and seeing no results. I had been in the studio almost every day for years, with nothing to show for it. I felt that it was all in vain and my work was going unnoticed. So she invited me to come out to dinner with her family, and I definitely wanted to go. I was so stressed out, I just wanted to feel human again. But I wasn't happy with my life, so I decided to suck up my feelings, stay at the studio, and keep working.

They had already chosen the first single, which was called "Dance For Me." Dr. Dre had sent tracks to write to, so we all listened to them a few times, finally agreed on the same track, and wrote the remix together. The next day we received a phone call. Mary loved it and had us come to The Quad studio. I produced Mary's vocals as she recorded the song, while her whole family was there dancing in excitement. Once the song was completely done, they liked the remix so much that they decided to make it the actual single and renamed the song.

Remaining loyal to God, coming from a dysfunctional family, and being dropped from my record label to start my own family, God blessed me with "Family Affair," the accomplishment that I'd been praying and working so hard for. And now I was ready for love.

I reached out to Lelee a few times to thank her and to see if there was anything I could do to return the favor or show my appreciation. My management agreement was about to end and I wanted to reconsider signing to her management company. But she was focused on what she was doing, which was understandable and respectable because she had her own situations going on. When we did finally speak, Lelee said, "Don't thank me. Thank God because as I help people, He always helps me." And that mind-set is what I've always respected about Lelee. We didn't speak much, but when we did, we'd talk for hours, sometimes about music, other times about love, relationships, crushes, and sex. That was our thing, and it always made sense because the two driving forces in my life were *love* and *music*.

I had my dream wedding. I had missed my high school prom because I was always at the studio. So I went all out, played dress up, and had a fantastic time. What made it beautiful to me was that it wasn't only about me. I incorporated his vision as well. I picked his brains to see what he liked and made sure that he was equally happy. I've never been the *me, me, me* type of girl. I never even had a honeymoon because my husband had to leave for Los Angeles the next morning. But what more could I have asked for? I was already living my dreams—*love* and *music*. Love was official—I had my dream wedding. And music was official—I had just co-written one of Mary J. Blige's biggest records ever, which crossed her over to the pop charts. I was happy, and I was tired. I didn't mind staying home and sleeping the whole day after my wedding.

Not long after getting married, we moved to Fresh Meadows, Queens. It was time to live on our own together, away from family and friends— far enough for privacy, but close enough to stay connected. We wanted them to come visit every so often, but this was our first time living on our own, so it kind of felt good to enjoy each other with no interruptions.

We were compatible. *I loved me some him!* And what made it so beautiful was that *he loved him some me* too! Being a wife and mother was the best job ever. It feels so good for me to have someone to make happy. I was able to create the kind of environment for my family that I wish I'd had growing up. My son went to a diverse school because I wanted him to know how to communicate with other races. The neighborhood was safe; my god kids, nephews, and nieces came over often. Our families had a place to come whenever they wanted to visit. We were doing really well for a long time.

We had been through everything you could imagine that couples go through: both having a record deal, both being dropped by our record companies, both having lots of money at the same time, both being broke at the same time, him with money and me with none, me with money and him with none, him cheating on me, me cheating on him, both having issues with each other's families. And we conquered it all because our love was bigger than the problems. When the love is strong, it doesn't matter what kind of storms hit; that love will still be standing after the storm.

The only problem is, there's a thin line between love and hate. Problems come all the time. Everybody in the world has problems. Life comes with problems, but sometimes the problems cause insecurities and the insecurities become a distraction from the love. When the problems become bigger than the love, the storm will blow you to the other side of the line before you even know it. I found myself fighting to stand on love's side. I didn't want to cross that line. Once a good girl's gone, she's gone forever. That's why we fight so hard. That's why we become nags. That's why we try to communicate and show our men what we feel. Our feelings allow us to know what's happening before it happens, so before it all falls down we're trying to catch it, pick it up, and step back on the side of love.

Many women have told me that I was lucky to be married, and that they couldn't wait until they were married. When I asked them why they wanted to be married, the answers were shocking. Some wanted to be married just for the title; others, for fear of being lonely. Many people don't think about the work required to maintain a marriage or what they need to bring to the table. They're just thinking about what they want from the table. Many people want someone to take them out of their misery and make them happy. But if you're not happy with yourself, then a relationship is the last thing you should be in. It's not nice to share your misery with others, or to expect someone to pull you out of your misery. That is *self-work* that you should take ownership of and work on so you can bring happiness to the table. Things happen, and when you're already involved in a relationship, naturally, you're supposed to do what you can to help and support each other. But it's challenging to help someone if they're not helping themselves.

Before you even invite someone into your world to share the rest of your life, make sure your world is a safe place—emotionally, physically, intellectually, occupationally, spiritually, and socially. If you meet someone that you're attracted to before you're fully accomplished, pay attention and see if it's someone you can build these things with before you "fall" in love. Most of us aren't established 100 percent in every area when we start to date. But if you see potential in each other, you can walk into the relationship together and build with each other, consciously standing on the side of the line with love together—by choice, not by default, by accident or by "falling." People in successful relationships support each other in reaching these goals. Many people pursue relationships because of physical attraction, or emotional attachment, or consistent sex. But they don't think about the reason why they should come together as one, their purpose with each other, their goals, and how they'd be living their lives together.

Once upon a time, I had a dream. That dream was to escape my miserable reality and create a life that would make me happy. I found happiness in music, so I didn't really have the urge to get married. Music always makes me happy. A broken marriage wouldn't make me happy. I'd prefer to be single and happy than married and miserable. I don't only dream about making lots of money, exotic cars, beautiful houses, traveling to places all over the world, or big weddings. I dream about love. I found love in creating music, as well as listening to music others have created. But when the love from a man came my way, I gave it a try. Love and marriage is a beautiful thing together, but when I could no longer feel the love, I couldn't understand the point of the marriage.

Marriage is "till death do you part." When the love died, the marriage was dead. It was the love that brought life to my marriage. Marriage had become a title, a piece of paper, and control. That's not what I was looking for. Love was the dream.

CHAPTER 3

Go Green

In a relationship, both people should be happy with themselves or at least know that it's their responsibility to work on their own happiness. When you totally depend on someone else to make you happy, it puts a lot of pressure on the other person. They start to lose themselves trying to be who you need them to be.

When you put expectations on someone you love, make sure they're realistic expectations and not too heavy a burden for someone else to carry. When you place your own responsibilities on someone else in a relationship, it can take away from what the other person should be doing to handle their own responsibilities. Everyone is supposed to sustain their own life first, and then come together. That's how the love stays vivid and alive.

From young, we all begin to develop our own perceptions of life. A female walks in her own lane, and has her own views. She envisions the kind of woman she wants to be, the kind of man she wants to be in it with her, and her expectations of him. Same thing for men. There are certain things that boys have to do for themselves in the process of becoming men. There are certain things a man may need to accomplish in order to feel confident, stand his ground, and be secure in his own lane before he's ready to commit and share his world.

If you're single, not looking for a relationship, and are happy that way, then staying in your own lane, standing your ground, being who you are, doing what you do, and staying true to yourself is what you should do—proudly and honestly. Don't make others think you want a relationship when you know you don't or aren't ready. But if you know deep down inside that you want or need companionship, or you have that burning desire for romance, or you have a strong passion for sex—if you're looking for consistency, and you know you really want a relationship—then you have to understand that it takes equal effort from both people to mix and make great chemistry. Too much of one and not enough of the other can cause an explosion.

Don't believe me? Just watch! Pay attention to an angry woman. Often, they're giving more then they're getting, overextending themselves, crossing the line, giving 70 percent when the other person is giving 30 percent.

At one point, in my relationship we were both giving fifty-fifty. After a while, when I came to the middle to mix I noticed he wasn't there. He actually pulled me into his *man cave* because he wanted to be together. And I went—knowing that I was crossing the line because I wanted to be together too. But the problem was that I didn't belong there. It was unnatural for me because I'm not a man and that's not my lane. Forgetting about me, and what I'm supposed to be doing, I neglected my own lane just to accompany him in his lane. It got really heavy for me, carrying all of his duties, and trying to pick up all the pieces that life knocked down and broke on his floor. It was his responsibility, because it happened in his lane. After realizing that it was too much for me, I'd go back to my lane and wait patiently for him to come pay me a visit, or at least meet me in the middle, where he belonged.

Sometimes, it happens the other way, too. Women want men to go all the way into their world. They may have a vision of the life they want, and when they find the perfect man to play the husband role, they try to change him and pull him into their world, but it's too much for him. He could lose himself because he doesn't belong there. We have to compromise and come out of our own lanes and meet in the middle. A man shouldn't have to cross the middle lane and come all the way to a woman's world. It might feel good to the woman, but it won't feel good to him. He won't be totally happy after a while. Let him be a man. He'll come to the middle after he sustains his own lane.

In the traffic laws of life, green means go! If a woman is yellow and a man is blue, the only way to become green and move forward is if they take equal steps from their own lanes and meet in the middle. The combination of yellow and blue is amazing. When a man and a woman meet in the middle, they've hit the jackpot. That perfect combination feels like money, and money is green. So, green is the objective for a successful relationship. Green is healthy, and health is wealth! Go green!

A woman's yellow world may be too bright and peachy for a man, and a man's blue world may be too dark and dull for a woman. But when they come together, they're green—not too bright, not too dark. Green is teamwork. It means you're both doing your jobs. It takes a woman and a man to put in equal effort—just like mixing the colors yellow and blue. Yellow can't be green without blue, and blue can't be green without yellow. Only together do yellow and blue make green.

Also, sometimes when people combine, they find they don't have good chemistry—like Clorox and ammonia. Not everything, or everybody, will mix well. Many times we see the signs, and we still try to force things that don't fit. That's why a lot of relationships don't last. If something happens naturally, let it happen, but if you have to dissect it, take it apart, pick it, pull it, push it, put it back together again, roll on the floor, do jumping jacks, shoot it, and bring it back to life, and it still doesn't work—you're probably better off leaving it in its own lane. Some blue things just want to stay blue, and some yellow things need to remain yellow. Great relationships start with *self*: knowing who you are and what you really want out of life; knowing the type of lifestyle you want for yourself and your family. If you know who you are, you'll have a better chance of attracting what you're looking for. If you're looking for someone else to make you happy but haven't found happiness within yourself, you may never find true and consistent happiness. Some people literally pull other people into their lanes. You shouldn't have to do that to be happy. You should be happy in your own lane first, and then walk from your lane into the middle and stop right there! If it's meant to be, the other person will be at that line also. As long as you don't cross the line, you won't lose yourself and get angry for overextending yourself.

This is the same for friendships, business partnerships, and all kinds of relationships. We share this world together. If everyone did their part, worked on themselves, and planted their feet on solid ground in their own lanes, then we could meet in the middle, life would be a green light, and we could all move forward together.

Sometimes people don't come to the middle because they're still working on their own situations. They may not be ready to go. Work on yourself first. Then, meet your partner in the middle. That's also how God works. God wants you to meet him halfway. You have to do your part first, and then God will take you places you can't go on your own.

Once you're secure in your own lane, then you can confidently meet your partner in the middle, and together you can go places that you probably would never even be able to imagine. God will not come and pull you off the couch. God helps those who help themselves. A partner should not have to come and pull you out of your lane. If you find yourself in someone else's lane trying to pull them into yours, or you're in the middle waiting for someone to meet you, they're probably still doing some self-work. Be patient! If there's no change, maybe they're on a different page than you. Maybe they're not willing to meet you halfway. Maybe they're walking down another lane. Maybe they realized that they wouldn't mix well with you. Sustain your own lane, just in case they never come to the middle. You should be happy in your own lane. Just leave it alone. It's that simple. Sometimes, people need a little pull. It's fine to step into someone else's lane just to help bring them into the middle, but if you're there far longer than you're supposed to be, naturally you may start to lose sight of yourself. Use your judgment and be strong enough to box with the punches that come your way when it's worth the fight to hold onto a relationship. But be wise enough to know when the efforts don't match and it's not worth the fight—and let go.

CHAPTER 4

When a Man Speaks, Listen!

One night, I was sitting in my living watching a movie. My son was asleep, the house was clean, dinner was already served, and candles were lit. Video games were the theme upstairs in the man cave, while I was downstairs alone wishing I had a man.

Fantasizing about love had become my regular routine since it was absent in my home. It was a new day, and as long as he and I were together, I felt compelled to keep trying. I had become the wife he needed me to be. He was number one on my priority list. I had a friendship feud with my girlfriends because of that. That's just how we were! It's a girl code. Before, we would never put a man before our friendship, but once you get married, things change. The man who marries you is now deserving of your full attention or at least should come before friends.

I'm not one to have unrealistic expectations, but because I was now his wife, I did expect my efforts to be reciprocated. I needed him to be my husband. His friends came over whenever they wanted and stayed however long they wanted. I had the right to express myself, so I waited for his friends to leave, went upstairs, sat down next to him, and said, "I need you. Can we spend some time together? I've been feeling lonely lately. I feel like I'm single, and you're right here."

He looked at me, got up, walked over to the light switch, turned it off, and said, "Turn your feelings off just like the light switch." Then he sat back down and began to play his video games again. I looked at him for about thirty seconds before I picked myself up and walked right back down the stairs, alone. Usually, I have an answer for everything. I remember this day as if it were yesterday because it was a pivotal moment in my life. Things changed from the moment I knew it wasn't even worthwhile for me to respond. I cried all night—not only because I was hurt, but because I knew this was the beginning of our ending. I started talking less and paying attention more. When a man speaks, listen!

A few days later, I received a phone call from my partner, Janai. She was going through her own personal problems, so we both needed an escape from our situations. Music was always a great escape for us, allowing us to keep our heads above the water when the ocean got too deep to stand in. So I invited her to come to New York from Georgia and stay at my house for a week so we could work on some music together.

When we first saw each other, we hugged liked the sisters in the film *The Color Purple*. We talked, laughed, cried, wrote music, sang, jogged, fought over donuts, and made some great records together. This was the first time we had worked on music together since releasing our first self-titled album, *Sa-Deuce*. We missed each other and had a lot of catching up to do. Our ability to be creative and turn our pain into pursuing our passion was a gift we both equally shared. For the most part we didn't even remember the hurt we had endured from our own personal circumstances. We were too glad to be working, to be mad about what wasn't working out in our relationships. Before we were both married, we had been equally focused on dreaming about our lives—not living in a fantasy world, but working towards living our dreams. We were dedicated, prepared to develop ourselves, and ready to work hard to make our dreams come true. We went to the studio, met with so many different producers, and had almost a full album of songs within a week. The problems I had with my husband were officially on hold. I prayed about them, and once I did, I didn't stress over them.

It was Janai's last night in New York and also her birthday, so I took her out to The Manhattan Proper for comedy night. We had a blast. Another thing Janai and I have in common is that we love to laugh.

A new comedian was hosting for the first time that night, and he was hilarious. Not just ordinary funny; he was funny to the point where we couldn't breathe—*falling-out-of-our-seats, holding-our-stomachs-from-the-pain-like-we-were-doing-crunches* type of funny. We had a good time. During our time together, we got some great songs done and had a few good laughs, so it was therapeutic for both of us.

As we got up to leave, I felt someone grab my arm. Not in a disrespectful way, but in a strong, protective, concerned way. He leaned over to me and put his mouth to my ear because the music was loud, and said, "What are you drinking?" in baritone.

I said, "Oh, I'm good. I was just about to leave, but thanks for the offer," and I tried to walk out. He gently held my hand and pulled me back toward him. I looked up and noticed it was the comedian. I said, "Oh my goodness, you were really hilarious!"

He picked up my hand and looked at the ring on my finger. And then he said, "Oh, you're married?"

I said, "Yes," as I tried to take my hand back and leave, but he held on. I said, "Listen, it's late, and I have to get up early, so have a good night."

He looked at me, but I was focused on the door and Janai, because she had to get her things together to leave in the morning. But this guy was very strong and aware. He stared into my eyes. I looked back and said, "Can I have my hand back?"

He then asked the million-dollar question: "Are you happy?"

I was speechless. For the first time in my life I felt so vulnerable. I needed love and affection. And I could definitely use some attention, since I was always the one giving it. I needed someone to notice me, but I wanted it from my husband. All I could do was replay his voice in my head saying, "Turn your feelings off, just like the light switch." I was so unhappy, but I didn't want anyone to know. I had been taught since I was young never to show my emotions. From the outside looking in, I seemed happy. But not many people came to me and asked if I really was—not even my own husband. I looked at this guy who had so much concern in his eyes. He looked at me and said, "What are you drinking?"

I looked at him with one of my blank stare expressions and said, "Apple martini."

Four apple martinis later, he became my new boyfriend. We had so much in common. He was married but legally separated and had already gone through what I was going through. He finished my sentences. He made me feel like the only woman in the establishment—until I looked up and saw Janai. She looked at me, and then at her watch. I already knew what that meant. I had to apologize because I had forgotten she was there. I forgot everyone else was there too. That night I had been reminded that there was life after death.

The truth is, my marriage was dead. We just weren't ready to accept it and move on. My love affair lasted for about six months before my husband found out. After a not-so-pretty scene, we decided to part ways and end the marriage. He left the house.

A week later, we spoke and set up a meeting to discuss the divorce. When he got to the house, he came with two bottles of wine. I found that to be quite interesting. I said, "You're treating me better now that you know you're getting rid of me, huh?"

He said, "Actually, I want to talk about what happened. I need to know what I did to make you do what you did." I explained everything to him. He didn't remember most of what he'd put me through, but I did. She who feels it knows it! He said, "I'm sorry. I don't know what I was thinking. I'm going through a lot and was so deep in my own thoughts. I'm sorry!" As he poured my third glass of wine, he started to remind me of the guy I'd met years before—humble, cool, smooth, caring, sensitive, attractive, secretly humorous, creative, and apologetic when he knew he was dead wrong. We started to kiss and the next thing I knew, we were "creatively vibing." Life was happening at home again. I decided to give love another try. We made some beautiful music that night. We created a big hit. I found out the following month that I was pregnant. That hit is what put us back on the charts.

We decided to try again. Going outside of my relationship wasn't the right thing to do. I owned that and apologized. I had thought our marriage was over. I had no right to do it, but it's so crazy what breezes the universe will blow our way to bring us to another level of awareness. Her name is Karma! Karma brings awareness in a more forceful way than when you don't want to take the scenic route. He miraculously began to hear my cries. I told him exactly what I needed from him and that I was lonely, before this could even happen. He didn't care to listen to me, and there was nothing I could do about it. I gracefully moved forward and trusted the universe.

Relationship Therapy: A man should listen to his woman. Don't take a woman for granted. Don't neglect your woman. I know it's cliché, but *what one man won't do, the next man will.* Women don't complain just for attention or to be nags. Most times, a woman is just being honest about something she really needs. A woman is like a plant. She's alive. Be aware that having a woman in your home means you have to nurture her, or else, just like a plant, she will die—not necessarily physically, but emotionally. Be aware of how powerful your words are.

He didn't mean to turn me off. He wanted me to turn my feelings off, but to be flexible and able to turn them back on when he wanted them on—but he hadn't said that part when he said those hurtful words months earlier. At that time, I did exactly what he said to do, because when a man speaks, I listen! I was truly turned off, but since the light bulb wasn't blown, he was able to turn me back on as soon as he came home.

I had a great pregnancy. We worked together to try to hold on to us, and for the sake of the kids we were able to pull it off and make it work. He was so present, in the moment, and caring.

But after I had the baby, things went right back to what had made us fall apart. This time it wasn't the things he said. When a man speaks, that's one thing—but actions speak so much louder.

CHAPTER 5

You Can't Make a Cat Bark

We all try to change others to be the way we want or need them to be. When you're in a relationship, change is good and actually necessary. For the efforts of both partners to match, the sense of urgency to work, learn, change, grow, and do for each other should be equal on both sides. As you expect certain things, you should be willing to give certain things as well, and this should be a cycle. A relationship takes a lot of work and honesty. When you love someone and you want to pursue a relationship, putting in the work should be a pleasure. You should naturally want to do the things necessary to make the other person happy. If you've already discussed and argued about an issue and there's still no change, the other person may have already made all the changes they'll ever make. The relationship may have run its course.

If you buy a puppy, knowing that it will grow into the pit bull you want in your home, then you should also know that you must train and take care of it. You want this puppy to be big, strong, and protective. You also want it to be smart, healthy, and a great companion—in other words, the best it can be. So you walk the puppy, feed it, give it water, and play-fight a little bit just to toughen it up. You give the dog a treat every time it shows some type of growth. You hug and love the dog.

Months go by, and the puppy is getting big now. It looks like a fully grown pit bull, but you've still never heard this dog bark. You're concerned, so you tease it, and try all kinds of things to get a *bark* reaction, because that's what dogs do—they bark. So, you start paying attention, and looking closely, you realize that the dog you thought you had isn't a dog. It's a cat—an exotic cat that looks, walks, and eats like a dog. But regardless of how much it may look like a dog, you can't make a cat bark!

People are who they are. You can't change them, just as you can't make a cat bark. You can only decide whether a particular person is the type that will work with your needs. A woman isn't always right, and for the record, we do not think we know everything; we *know* we don't. But a real woman in love will figure it out when it's worth it, and she won't stop until her man is happy. There's no perfect man, but if one is open to growth and willing to learn, work and elevate, then that's *imperfectly perfect,* and that's all she needs. Pride and ego will stunt your growth and can make you think you're barking when you're just aggressively or destructively meowing!

You may need to date or be in a relationship to find out more about yourself. A lot of us think we can make a relationship work until we're put in the situation and realize we're not ready. That's okay! It's only human. This is why it's good to date first and nurture a relationship before you jump into something serious. You start making promises and becoming attached and then things change. Someone might require you to do something you're not even equipped to do. The purpose of such a relationship might be to show you that you have more growing to do on your own before you can commit. What you just found out about life today your date may have found out three years ago. For that person to be in a relationship with you would be like going back and starting the last three years over again.

In relationships people are basically mirroring each other, because if we stand up on our own, we can't see ourselves. When we allow others to get close to us, we are trusting them to see personal things about us. We're supposed to encourage and help each other grow. We should inspire, lift up, teach, and feed each other daily. We shouldn't judge each other when we fall, but put our hands out and pull each other back up, and then continue walking side by side, stepping up the ladder of life together. That ladder has steps. If you're willing to keep stepping up, but your partner wants to stop, you have to make a major decision: Will you be okay standing on the same step with your partner, or do you need forward continuity in your life? If you bought a cat by accident but you really wanted a dog, it's up to you to be honest with yourself. If you like animals and it really doesn't matter that you have a cat—you're already attached and you're cool with what you have—then, fine. Keep the cat and accept it for what it is, meows and all. But if you know you need a dog, and you're keeping the cat and trying get it to bark because you got attached and don't want to let it go, you may live a miserable life—you and your cat that will never be able to bark!

The best relationships happen when we know and love ourselves first. That allows us to be honest and realize when something won't work. Know the difference between being attracted, being attached, and being equally yoked.

I moved to Georgia not long after my daughter was born, with the intention of starting anew. I needed some time to figure things out. I felt neglected and unsupported at home, yet pressured to live up to certain expectations. Meanwhile, I had a male friend who was very supportive and gave me everything I needed, but whom I couldn't even build with because I was married. I needed to get away from both of them, to be honest.

My New Year's resolution in January of 2006 was to discontinue any and every relationship that was in motion by default. From the beginning of that year, my love affair had already been over. In February, I decided to try to save my marriage when my daughter was conceived. It wasn't my intention to start something new in the midst of the madness before ending an old thing, but it happened, and I went with the flow. I made the decision to *stop* going with the flow and to start creating and building the type of relationships that I actually wanted. Being with my husband was also *going with the flow,* because I knew we weren't equally yoked. However, I let it continue to happen, and could only hope and pray that things would change for the better.

A few months after going to Georgia to get some clarity, I realized it would be a great place to raise a family. It was beautiful. The kids had more than enough land to run and be free. They'd go swimming in our subdivision peacefully with the other kids. The energy in Georgia was *peachy*—much more relaxed than the Big Apple where we came from. I wanted the kids to experience this with their father also, so for the sake of keeping the family together, we tried again.

After a year in Georgia, I got the clarity I needed. It's not easy to walk away from someone you truly love, but when God shows you clear signs about your relationship and gives you a way to escape, it's your responsibility to acknowledge the signs. I had been through so much pain that had left me numb, and through that whole metamorphosis period I was forced to grow. It was easier for me to see things as they were in my relationship rather than how I wanted them to be. Not everyone is equipped to be married. Marriage is not for people who refuse to consider that their behavior may negatively affect the people close to them. If someone wants to stay the way they are and doesn't feel the need to make changes for the better, there's no point in being married. There was no change, and I wasn't happy, because I was settling. By settling for something I knew wasn't right for me, I had created my own unhappiness.

CHAPTER 6

That Thin Line

There I was again, this time not on my knees but on my face, asking God, "Now, what?" I asked God to lead me in the direction He wanted me to go in, and to surround me with the people I needed to be around to find my purpose. God moves in mysterious ways, and never ceases to amaze me. My sister, the one who knew how to dodge the drama when we were younger, who didn't want to bring me with her because she'd be raining on her own parade, had become my umbrella. She was very instrumental to me and my kids while I was going through the storm. Regaining a sense of self after being with someone for so long isn't easy. I lost so many friends. I received destructive and negative attacks. People I thought were my friends were maliciously doing things to sabotage my relationships and goals. I got constant complaints about *what I wasn't doing for them.* Trusting God and remaining on the road of forward continuity was the only way I chose to move.

Erin, the original light-skinned girl from our group 4 Shades of Black, who moved away in high school, moved back to New York. "What's going on with you?" she would ask. "What's your next move?" "Why don't you have a song on the Billboard charts right now?" I told her my story, she told me hers. We shed tears, and began to discuss ideas. While I was in New York working my creative side and pursuing music, she had gone to college in Atlanta, majored in business with a background in finance, graduated with a BA degree, and had already run a few major companies. Timing is everything. I needed a new team. I was all over the place. I was depressed and trying to recover from losing my marriage, losing friends that I thought were on my team, and losing my father to cancer.

My other friend, Joanne from high school, would also reach out to me, but many times I wasn't too responsive because I was trying to figure my life out. Whenever we did speak she never complained, but was more curious as to why I was so standoffish. I told her my story, she told me hers. And, she invited me to her house for a ladies' night, where I met other women who were ready to discuss building a business together over some home-cooked food and beverages.

Erin and Joanne were both women going through their own personal situations. Whenever we got the opportunity we'd come together to share ideas and expand on life. Money can't buy happiness, but supporting each other, setting goals, and working toward them was therapeutic for me. It allowed me to again dream my life and start working toward living my dreams, instead of basking in my reality of unfortunate events.

We planned a trip and went to a women's conference in Atlantic City. It was nothing short of purposeful that we ran into Ma Barker at the conference. She is the one who had introduced me to Erin in High School. After sharing the same space and hearing so many successful women speak, I came back to New York renewed.

Being at home with no husband, no son (because he had left for college), and a daughter who was in school during the day, I finally found time for me. In spending more time with myself, I began to truly love myself and understand how to accept my flaws. I asked myself things like, *What would it feel like to do for myself everything that I've been doing for everybody else? And if I did, how much closer would I be to finding my purpose in life?* And also, *Am I happy?* In being true to yourself, you must have a lot of courage. You may have to say no a little more often to others. *No* is a very powerful word! Not only did I want to be honest with myself, I was also curious: Who are my real friends? Who actually loves me for me and supports me? Who would still be around for me if

I decided to be honest, and do what I can when I can, but say no when I sincerely can't? Who are the ones that actually applaud me when I win?

Spending time with me, I discovered that I had spent much of my life living the way other people wanted me to. There's nothing wrong with doing for others, compromising, supporting others, and being there for loved ones. But I learned the hard way that if you're not in a place where you can realistically do things for others, It can be dangerous for your own well-being. I don't give to get. I don't expect my loved ones to give back just because I gave. I give what I can naturally, and I'm totally cool if all you have to give is love, appreciation, and happiness. I'm a firm believer that the universe will bless me with the things I need once I do the right things and handle my responsibilities.

I lived a great part of my life conforming and being the person society wanted me to be—holding back on who I really am just to be relatable and likable to my peers. I was *the cool kid* when I was who everyone wanted me to be. But the problem was that I wasn't cool with me, because I wasn't who I wanted me to be. Once I started spending more time with myself, meditating as well as praying, I started to feel free. I have so many gifts that I had shelved in the closet, along with lots of baggage because of insecurities. Being home alone, I started to clean up. I felt like a gay kid ready to come of the closet. No secrets, no lies, just me finally accepting me.

Where I came from, being confident was taboo. It was often mistaken for being conceited or cocky, so subconsciously I began to develop a fear of appearing un-relatable and superior. Most people thrived on the insecurities of others, so I had very few faithful and fearless people around me who understood me, pushed me, and encouraged me to follow my dreams. Tracey, my very first best friend, was one of those few. She came from a household in which her father didn't allow anyone to slack. He would often lecture people about going to college. I got a pass, because he knew that music was my passion. So he'd push me to follow through with my dreams. His mind-set was that of a *rich dad*, in contrast to my *poor dad*'s. My father used to yell at me if he caught me singing in the mirror and would tell me to stop showing off. Tracey's father encouraged me to show my voice off. I don't remember my father ever telling me that I had a nice voice. He discussed all the reasons why I should not sing professionally. Tracey's mother had tears in her eyes when I sang. They used to watch The Grammy Awards on TV, and I would be right there in their house watching with them. That's where they wanted to see me, and that's where I wanted to be. Because my parents were religious, we never did things like that together at home.

Many people that know me by my first name, Paula, made fun of me when I renamed myself Asiah. Very few understood or supported my new name. *Asiah* is my alter ego—my fearless side, the side that is confident, that doesn't hold back, and believes in living her dreams. *Paula*, the person born because of her parents' choices, was damaged, rough, tough, and didn't believe her dreams were valid. Never fully accepted. Judged. Hated! Unfortunately, I didn't have enough people around me with the faithful mind-set, so I had to be Paula more than Asiah. I love Paula. She's my foundation and the girl that throws her hands up when she feels she's being backed into a corner. Paula's got my back and will fight for me, but Asiah feels as though she shouldn't have to fight. Asiah is super-creative, talented, driven, and wants to create a life in which her fantasy becomes reality. Her confidence level is so high that she really believes these fantasies are realistic and obtainable. She doesn't fantasize about having wings and flying in the skies, taking breaks and chilling on the clouds, doing backflips off tall buildings in New York City, or swimming in the oceans of Anguilla as a mermaid. Asiah has dreams that she sincerely feels can come true. Paula's dreams were totally crushed. Paula and Asiah were always in a battle. Paula loves to eat all kinds of food; she gains a lot of weight, hates makeup, loves sweatpants and boxers in the house and Nikes on the streets. Asiah works off all the food that Paula eats, likes to be fit, and dresses as if she's on the red carpet. She loves to wear makeup and different colors of lipstick to match her hair, nails, shoes, bags, belts, high heels, and cars. Asiah doesn't want to be on the streets, she wants to live her dreams. Spending time alone allowed Paula and Asiah to come together as one, and realize that they are both equally significant. Together, I am very well-balanced.

Paula had experienced a high level of hate since the second grade. That was my first and only year going to public school, and then in third grade I went back to private school and it happened again. The girls in these schools didn't even know each other, but they acted the same. One minute we were having a good time, cheerleading, playing double Dutch, singing songs, and dancing in the locker room as if we were on stage, and the next minute they all weren't my friends. *Like, how does this stuff happen? Did they plan this together? Did I do something wrong? Can I get an explanation?* That affected me; even though I was taught never to show emotions, it hurt so much inside. As I grew up, it didn't stop. Even with the ones that I've allowed myself to get close to because I trusted, and thought understood me. I realized that it's just human nature.

I've always felt the hate. Not for being the prettiest, or the richest, or the most talented, or the best, but for having the courage to believe in myself and stand strong, even if that meant I had to stand alone. Because I am human, it did bother me, so from time to time that fear would kick in—the fear of being un-liked and unaccepted. I found myself holding back because I cared about what others thought. I couldn't be fully myself if I wanted to have friends, so I had to hold back just to fit in. But when I was home or had the opportunity to be alone, I would dream. I hated the life that I was born into, but I loved the people that I'd met in it. I love my family and friends, but I hated the life that was given to us as minorities. And I hated the fact that everyone seemed to be cool living that lifestyle. We deserve more! But I always seemed too crazy for people. I always felt that my hopes and dreams for us as a people were too big. It wasn't about wanting more money because my family was always broke; I knew how to get around, survive and be happy with no money. I wasn't just looking for a paycheck, because everyone spent so much time working hard for that check, but once they paid their bills, they were still unhappy, complaining that they were broke all over again. I wanted a whole new way of living. It was never only about the check for me, it was always about the lifestyle.

Being alone allowed me to envision, but when you allow yourself to get close to others, naturally they want their feelings to be your feelings, their problems your problems, and their misery your misery. As human beings, we all have down days, so yes, it absolutely feels good to have friends who understand how you feel and can be supportive because they can empathize and relate. But what happens if you get your life together and you're not miserable anymore? Does misery love happiness too? I don't deal with my misery by attaching myself to other miserable people. I find that when I pray and turn my misery over to God, I'm not miserable anymore—I'm happy. I thank God every time I get the chance for being this way. I may not have the smallest waist or the prettiest face, but I have a lot of faith. Happiness loves company also, and I learned how to love myself enough to surround myself with other happy people. It's very important that you know your surroundings. I'm very passionate about living my dreams. That doesn't mean that the people I've allowed myself to get close to have the same passion for their dreams. You can't do epic things with basic people, and I expect great things, so I choose to surround myself with people who understand that. The people who don't understand it see things in a totally contrary way. They think I'm crazy; they complain about everything I do or don't do, and then they become a big distraction.

I know many people that I love dearly, and that love me too, who are happy with a basic lifestyle. I'll spend time with them, eat, play cards, watch movies, and socialize. When it's time for me to leave, we hug, say our good-byes, and wish each other happiness and good health—no bridges burned. We stay connected. That's love, right there. We stay connected because we love and respect each other. Nothing else matters.

But then, there are those that don't want you to leave. They want you to stay with them. Some people actually get mad at you for leaving. Some people make it a big deal and feel that you're not being a good, supportive friend if you have to leave—as if you don't have your own things to do. Now, that's not love. That's fear, loneliness, insecurity. That's on the other side of the love line! Their reaction shows that these people are not really happy with themselves. They're not okay having to dealing with their own situations. They may have personal issues holding them back, so they get mad at *you* for being who you are, being fearless, and doing what you must for yourself.

Being fearless isn't a bad thing, but people can make you feel as if it is. Fearlessness is godliness, because when you *fear less*, it's because you're full of faith. You believe everything will be okay if you do what you need to for yourself. You trust God!

You are the author of your own story, you are the director of your own movie, you are the DJ for the music you choose to play in your own home, you are the creator for your own life. If you could live the way you really wanted to, how would you live? Sometimes we become slaves to people around us, feeling obligated to do things we really don't want to do. Being afraid of losing close people is not a good way to live. If you lose people because you decided to get your life together and focus on the person you're becoming and take more control of your life, then perhaps those you lost were too close anyway. We need our personal space to grow and maintain our own individuality. There's a difference between close friends and real friends. The real ones don't need to be too close. Real friends understand that you need your space and they respect it. The real ones will be there no matter what. They won't burn bridges even when there are differences. When differences occur, they're free to fall back and keep to themselves, but real friends won't hate you because of them. Love builds bridges that allow us to cross over to stay connected with each other. Confident people know that no matter where in the world you are, there's still some bridge that they can cross to come see you and share love. Insecure people don't see things this way. Once they think they're about to lose you they start to panic, and they don't always see things clearly. They don't see the bridge so they feel they're losing control of you. They act up, start to trip, and then fall, for no real reason. Some people want to be so close that no bridge is required, but as individuals, we should be able to stand on our own. Some people want to be close because they seek to control you. They'll try to get close enough to figure you out and learn your every move, close enough to reach you and pull you back down when they see you're trying to come up. That's insecurity, and fear of being left behind.

Do what you can for the people you love, but if saying yes to someone contradicts your identity and beliefs, you don't have to be bullied into doing anything for anyone against your wishes. Faith and fear live right across the street from each other. They are so close! One minute, someone may love you and have faith in your relationship. But then before they even realize it, they're standing on the side with fear, and that's where the hate starts to kick in. There's a thin line between faith and fear. Fear is a liar. It makes false evidence appear real. When you're in fear, it's hard to see the truth and stand on the other side of the line in faith.

You know that thin line between love and hate? That line is so thin that sometimes the ones who really love you don't even realize they're standing on the other side, hating. People get attached, and start having expectations and perceptions of you. They develop a vision of the role they want you to play in their lives. But what about you, your perceptions, your dreams? If your biggest dreams are their worst nightmares, you may need new people. They might not be the right people to surround your self with. Those that want to get close to you because of insecurities will do everything in their power to sabotage and destroy what you've worked so hard to build.

Spending time alone, I had to be honest with myself. I had to check myself and do some major soul searching. I've been accused of a lot of things. Change is necessary when you're growing and positioning yourself for new opportunities. But people will point fingers at you, fault you for everything, and turn minor errors into big problems. It's as if their feelings are in 3-D, and they only feel what they feel, so they can't be supportive when you need them to be happy for you. Some of these people who've crossed that thin line obviously came from the other side, which means they may have once loved you. It's always good to do self-evaluation, to see if there is any truth when people accuse you of something—especially when you love them, too. If you're guilty of something, own it! Be strong. Apologize for anything you did that may have been wrong or hurtful. But if things don't add up, and you've checked and changed yourself, and you're still being misjudged and wrongfully blamed, and you don't receive any apologies—forgive them and walk away. Actually, run like Forrest! There are many people that I've never received apologies from to whom I've apologized just to keep the peace. They may never apologize. I've forgiven them anyway, and kept it moving, because I need to be free to live my life. I have things to do, people to see, places to go, kids to raise, and dreams to fulfill. But blame games and pity parties are events I choose not to attend anymore. I party with a purpose!

Once I knew my worth, I found it worthless to be around people who don't. I decided to stop acting as if I don't feel the hate from those who hate me. Can't we all just get along? Black people who hate on other black people just because of personal differences are no different than other races who judge others based on racial differences. When you have goals and dreams that haters can't destroy, they will tarnish your name and character. Surround yourself with those who allow you to be yourself and will respect you for being different—whether you're gay, straight, black, white, an artist, the president, corporate, Indian, Asian, African, Haitian, Jamaican, light-skinned, dark-skinned, blue, green, a male ballerina, or a female engineer.

Where I come from, we hold on to old relationships out of fear of losing each other and fear of being disloyal, which means that to make each other comfortable we have to remain somewhat relatable. People grow and people change. If someone can't love you for who you are or who you've become and accept your differences, then it's better to let them hate you for choosing to not to be who they want you to be. Let it go. Let the old relationships die, because there is life after death. Dream about the life you want to live. Start a new life. Dream your life. There's nothing wrong with that, as long as you're not sleeping. Wake up and live your dreams.

Some people take the phrase *be who you really are* out of context. It doesn't give permission to disrespect people, just because that's what you want to do. Relationships are very important. Nobody really wants to let go of relationships that were once good if they don't have to. Do your part, check yourself, and make changes. Be your best self—not your worst self. We all have the best and worst of both worlds in us, but none of us is in this world alone. We are all *earth-mates* and should consider that other people share this world with us. If you live in the same house with another person, you're roommates. If you're in the same class at school, you're classmates. If you're compatible friends or lovers, you may be soul mates. Whatever type of mate you may be, be considerate.

That thin line is very important. It's there for a good reason. Figure out which side of the line you want to stand on. When you love and hate someone at the same time, that is confusion and can be destructive. If you know you hate someone, stop trying to hold on. Hate them and stay away, but if you're going to love someone, love them. Get rid of the hate, but don't try to stand on two grounds. Some people keep one foot on one side, the other foot on the other side, and go back and forth. That causes a lot of drama. Choose a side and stick to it. I say choose love! Love is understanding, patience, faithful, fun, confidence, and happiness. But on the other side of that line is hate, lack of forgiveness, anger, control, possessiveness, grudge-holding, and unhappiness. Which ground are you standing on? Ask yourself this question. Break yourself down, and then build yourself back up. Once you've done that, then no one should be able to break you down because you've already done it to yourself. I had to build myself back up when I hit rock bottom. I don't have time or any reason to hate anyone, because I try my best to live with purpose and understanding. I believe there's a reason for everything, so I'm always searching for the reasons so I won't have to hate. I'm a big dreamer, but I am also a big doer once I have sight, vision, and confirmation from God on what I should be doing. If I don't have a vision or can't really see my future, it's nobody else's fault. It's my responsibility to figure it out. It's your job to do the same. Go where you need to go, be where you need to be, and see who you need to see to be who you need to be. I am living proof that dreams do come true if you're loyal and faithful to them.

CHAPTER 7

The Best Things in Life Are Created

Throughout the various stages in my life, I've met many different people. The reason I'm able to maintain sincere relationships is that I see people for who they are and accept them. No deception. God made us all. I see the good and the bad. I just choose to focus on the good. None of us is perfect. I'm far from it. Everybody in the world has problems. But I find it most amazing when we can come together and explore the many beautiful things about each other and win together *because* of our problems. It hurts my heart when others complain about the things they don't like about people, even if those things are real. My theory is: You can either *whine* or *win*. Personally, I'd rather win.

To win, you have to be creative. You must create the type of life you want. It's like painting a picture. I'm going to choose the colors that I like. If I don't like the colors, I won't use them. That's how I deal with people. I'm going to choose the things I like about you and use them to create a great life. The things I don't like I have no use for. They don't exist for this painting. It's that simple. They don't bother me at all. That's your business. God put us on this earth for a reason. We are supposed to help each other and use each other for our own life pictures. Yes, we are supposed to use each other! That's what we're here for, as long as we're not misusing each other.

I won't call my gynecologist if I'm going to the studio. I will not call my lawyer when I need to get my hair done. If I think someone I'm sexually intimate with is lying to me about a sexually transmitted disease, then my GYN is the one to call. She'll tell me the truth, but if I call my GYN to record my vocals and give it a nice mix at the studio, then I'm misusing her. That's not what she does. If I'm trying to paint a certain picture or create a certain life, I have to be strategic about the colors I use and the people I choose.

It's the same with all kinds of relationships. Sometimes we get so emotionally attached to people that we lose sight of our own visions, pictures, responsibilities, priorities, goals, and even our purpose. Sometimes, just because we're attached to people we want to put them on our team. That's not necessarily a good idea. It doesn't mean they're not good people, it just means we see who they are. If I need to vent—which, Lord knows, I do—I'll call my girlfriends, plan a ladies' night out, and catch up. If I'm feeling sexy, I don't want to call my girlfriends. I'm going to call the man that grinds my gears.

People are who they are. If we respected that, the life that we create for ourselves would probably come closer to the perception that we have in our heads. Life is what you create it to be. God is the original creator. He created us in His own image, so we, too, are creators. People create their own drama. Millionaires create their own financial success. I don't believe in luck. I believe in making wise choices. Do you want to whine, or do you really want to win? Some people feel comfortable whining. Maybe it's relaxing, but if you really are wondering what it takes to make your life better, be open to the solutions to the problems that are causing you to whine in the first place.

Once we know who we are and what we're looking for, life gets much better. Learn that you may never understand everything about everyone, but as long as you understand yourself, then it will be much easier to understand that others have *selves* too, which are different from you. When you understand this, you'll be able to get to know who others are. When you *become* the truth, you can see the truth.

When you meet someone and you both feel the same level of connection or attraction, it's better to get to know each other and understand each other's differences before you jump into bed together. If the passion is there, then it's worth it to start creating. Some people are so eager to jump into bed because they just want to have sex, but they don't put the time in to create. Sex with no passion is like jokes with no laughing, a model with no fashion, an athlete with no action, or checks with no cashing. It can happen, but it might not be good, and what's the point if it's not good enough to maintain? If you can't sustain it, is it really worth it?

Good sex is created just like good music. Sometimes freestyles work. You hear a beat that makes you immediately start to have feelings, and then you get in the booth and start recording various thoughts off the top of your head. That happens in the bed too. You can meet someone and instantly be attracted to each other and freestyle in the bedroom and the chemistry can be amazing. And yet, a lot of people are left brokenhearted and wonder why they don't have significant others. If all you want to do is freestyle, you may end up with a *one-hit wonder*. But if you want real love or to make good music, have a purpose, and a plan. Be honest—but be creative.

I've always compared love relationships to the music business. Signing a contract always felt like getting married to me. Many people want to work and freestyle, or go with the flow—until someone wants to sign them to their production, management, or record company. This is when things change. You find out who's serious, in it for the long run, ready to commit and give it all they have. Even when things start perfectly, you may get nervous and wonder if it's going to last. You may begin to wonder what their intentions were in wanting you to sign that paper. You want to be sure you're making the right choice for the long run, even when it feels good for the moment.

That feeling you get when you're feeling the same thing as someone else is orgasmic. I promise you, I'm not lying when I say making music can be just as good as making love. I've had more passionate music sessions in the studio than sex sessions in the bedroom (and vice versa, of course). It's about the passion, the chemistry and the willingness to put the work in to keep creating until you get it right. When two people are equally passionate about the same thing at the same time, they're going to make some really good love or some really great music. Creating in the studio is very intimate. This is the time to tap into your feelings and bring honesty and creativity to life. This is the perfect place to emote, and the best part is when the person you're creating with allows you to do so gracefully with no judgment, just open honesty with intentions to make it better. You have to make sure you allow in the right kind of energy so everyone's on the same page, feeling the same thing, and headed the same direction.

Music is life. Creating a song from scratch, writing, recording, packaging, releasing it, and watching it hit number one on the pop charts is like having sex, getting pregnant, giving birth, and then watching your child grow, go to college and live their own life. Music is life! Even if you never get a hit record on the charts, if you were able to get in the studio with the right energy, you've experienced something that feels like sex. If you've completed the song and were able to take it home and listen to what you've created, you've experienced that orgasmic feeling. If the song never got placed and was never released, then you didn't get to the pregnancy stage, but everyone knows that the creation process is the fun part. Seeing your kids grow is amazing, but so is having sex without pregnancy. Having a hit record is amazing, but so is being in the studio making records. Creating *love* or *music* definitely feels good. But, do you have a goal for what you're creating?

Before you have sex with someone, think about whether that person is worth creating with. Before many successful producers even allow anyone in their studios, they want to make sure the person is worthy: *Why are you here? Who sent you? What are you trying to do? How long have you been doing it? Whom do you know? Why should I work with you? How are you going to react when something happens that you don't like? Can you control your emotions? Are you levelheaded?* They ask all kinds of valid questions out of concern for security, and then it still takes time before they'll allow you in the studio. Yet, they'll allow you into their bedrooms in two-point-two seconds with no questions asked. People protect and respect their intimacy in the studio more than in the bedroom.

Love works the same way music does. If you're looking for love, ask the same questions. Your dates should be like job interviews, but with honesty and fun. You don't have to be politically correct, because when people spend time with you they will see if who you are matches who you *say* you are. So, just be honest. Life is what you create it to be. If you want to attract someone who is honest, you have to *be* honest. If your truth turns someone off, that's perfect. You just saved a lot of time and heartache, because you would've attracted the wrong person and found out when it was too late. You can create the type of family and lifestyle you want when you date. It's a choice. Finding a co-parent should not happen by accident. Your co-parent should be your lover, your life partner.

If you took the time to get to know someone before having sex, then you probably wouldn't have the urge to have sex with them anymore. I'm pretty sure that most people have had sex with someone and wished they could take it right back. Many people get caught up in the moment and the physical attraction, but later suffer the consequences. What if we inquired about the other person's mind and their *later*—rather than their *now*?

Where do they see themselves in five years? I need to know if it's anywhere close to the same place that I see myself in five years. If it is, you may be the next color I'd like to use for my painting. And with my truth and honesty, the other person would have the right to decide if I'm a color he'd like to use for *his* painting, because he has a reality that he's creating as well. It must be equal on both sides. If the visions are similar, there is potential. The creating process would be fun once you trust that each other's color choices make sense together and that you're headed the same direction.

It ignites my concern when I see someone that is still complaining today about the problems of yesterday. I wonder if it's just in their nature to complain and if they're actually fine with their life, or are they're really open for advice because they want change. Some people get mad when you give them real talk because they're comfortable in their regular patterns. Lately, I get confused when people complain. I find myself wondering if I should just sit there, keep my mouth closed and listen when I can clearly hear what the problem is, *or* offer a solution because I genuinely want to help. Over the years, I've learned to talk less and open my eyes and ears more. People will fight you when you tell them the truth, yet complain that you aren't *keeping it real* if you don't say anything.

Sometimes, people just want to hear themselves talk. But if they're constantly talking about the same problems without seeking advice to fix them, why should you have to sit there and suffer through that? If you find yourself lonelier around certain people than you are alone, you need new people. If you don't fit in, it's okay to walk away and stand out. Ask God to surround you with those who are right for you. Ask God for the courage to make the right choices and walk away from the wrong ones.

You have to create the kind of life you want, otherwise all kinds of things will happen to you—not because you have bad luck, but because you're available. Bad things happen often, and can happen to anyone, anywhere. If bad things had legs, they would jump all over every one of us—if we stood there and let them. You have to move around, stay busy! Don't put yourself in harm's way. Go where good things happen. Shake that bad stuff off. If you let it sink in too deep and it gets into your pores, even a shower can't wash it away.

When my life isn't going the way I want, that's because I'm not being responsible. My life, however, is amazing when I own it and take responsibility. Sometimes I need a cleansing. People will poison your mind with their problems and now they'll be stuck inside of you. But God may want something different to be on your mind so you can do His job and live your purpose. You may have gotten caught up in trying to be who everyone wants you to be—or who *they* told you that *you* should be. You'll never find yourself if you live for everyone else. It's okay to be different. You don't have to try to fit in. Figure it out. You only have one life to live. How are you living it? If we spent less time complaining about our lives and more time creating them, we'd actually enjoy it!

CHAPTER 8

Let Your Voice Be Heard

One of the biggest fears I had for a long time was the fear of other people's opinions. The things everyone else thought became bigger than my own thoughts, because there were always more of them than me. Their voices became louder than mine. I developed a lot of self-doubt and stood in my own way because of it. Whenever I was alone, though, I would listen to the sounds of my own voice. I realized that my thoughts and feelings are mine for a reason. I had to distance myself in order to let go of the self-doubt, because the voices in my own head were what I needed to hear to be sure of myself. Once I was able to grasp this concept, I stopped seeing myself through the eyes of people that don't even understand me, or my art. I found it worthless to listen to people who don't value me. They don't know my value, but I do. So it was up to me to start taking control of my own life.

People want to control you, but they can't even control themselves. That doesn't make any sense. If you want to change the world or anyone around you, you must start by changing yourself. Everyone has opinions that come out of their mouths, just as everyone has bowel movements that come out of their anal sphincters. Literally, people *talk crap*! Opinions can be just as toxic and poisonous as *number two*.

I began my journey as a signed recording artist, so I know what a true artist really needs. Many artists have the same fear I had, and because I'm aware of it, I'm sensitive to it. I see myself in other artists, and that's what made me want to start coaching. I know what I needed and what I wish I'd had. That's why I care so much about my clients. I want to give them what they need. I want to see the growth. I want to know that I made a difference in someone else's life. The voice flows so freely and authentically without the worries and fears of judgment. Because I'm not judgmental, my vocal clients begin to trust me. They know I'm not being destructive when I give my criticism, because I come with solutions and they see the results.

Fearless and *unique* is what you should be. No worries! I needed someone to advise me, show me the way, develop me, and teach me different ways of thinking and being. I needed someone to be honest with me, love me, push me, and support me whether I was right or wrong. I needed a hero. But after so many years of making mistakes and failing, I got stronger and wiser. I had become the person I was looking for. I wish I'd had someone to tell me when I was younger that it's okay to be the best I can be, regardless of what anyone thinks. I wish I'd had someone to tell me not to worry about the judgmental nature some people have. I wish I'd had someone to tell me how beautiful I was, and that it's okay to be me, confident. I knew I could sing, but I didn't know it was okay to have a voice. I finally found my voice, when I lost everybody else's. I had been focused on the wrong things—what everybody else thought. *What if I go off key or can't hit the high note? What if the music is too loud and I can't hear myself? I'm going to sound as if I can't sing. People are going to talk about me.* Thoughts like these are distracting. They'll make you nervous when you are trying to be the best you can be so you can make a difference in the lives of people who actually appreciate it. These insecure voices in my head were only distractions based on fear of other people's opinions, and they didn't go away until I stopped feeding them. Anything you feed will grow. If you feed your fears, they will grow. I decided to starve them, to pay them no attention. I decided to feed my dreams. I wanted to see how big they would grow and where they would take me. Why not? I already knew what it was like to feed into other people's crap and neglect myself. I sincerely wanted to see what would happen if I didn't. I definitely lost a lot of "friends" and off-pitch voices. Music is life. Part of it, should be in unison. Every voice, everyone you surround yourself with, should be on the same accord, same tone, same key, and same page. When we're ready to embrace our differences, it's time to live in harmony—different notes that blend consistently and orderly with pleasing arrangements of mutual relations. Otherwise, when the voices don't mix well, they clash and become noise—total chaos. Sometimes you have to tune out the noises of the world so you can hear your own voice.

Once you're sure of what the voices in your head are telling you, you become more confident. Confusion comes from hearing your own voice, listening to other voices, and going back and forth, letting other people have a negative effect on you.

Do you like the sound of your voice? It's your voice. You're supposed to love it. Listen to the tone you are using. The key word in my last sentence was *listen!* In order to have a pleasing voice, you should first be able to hear it. If you use your voice without even listening to yourself, your tone may be too loud, harsh, and dissatisfying. Finding your voice first requires having a good ear. Everybody wants to be heard. Let your voice be heard. That's what it's here for. But before you speak, listen! It's all about finding the right voice to use.

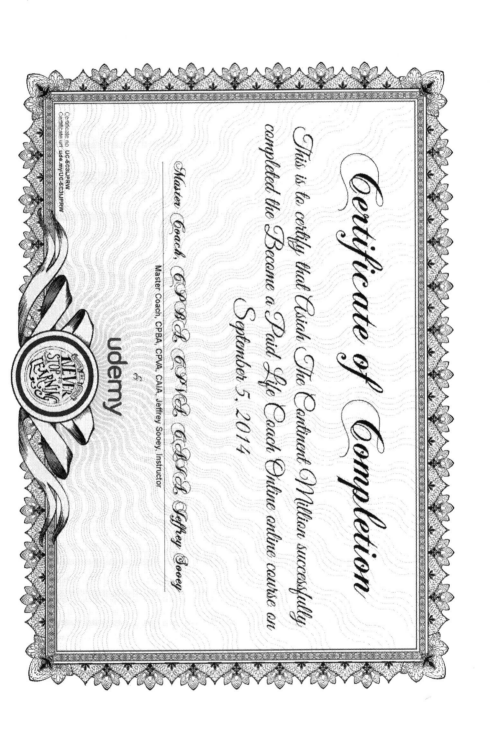

Certificate of Completion

This is to certify that Asiah The Continent Million successfully completed the Become a Paid Life Coach Online online course on

September 5, 2014

Master Coach, CPBA, CPVA, CAIA, Jeffrey Sooey

Master Coach, CPBA, CPVA, CAIA, Jeffrey Sooey, Instructor

udemy

NEVER STOP LEARNING

Certificate no   UC-5C3UPRW
Certificate url   udemy/UC-5C3UPRW

CHAPTER 9

The Greatest Gift of All

Many of us go to schools of the arts, join the rowing team, retain vocal coaches, practice sports, or go to other places to develop our gifts and skills. Some go back to school for higher learning and degree upgrades. What we do with our time is our choice. If we made the choice to use every minute of our time to search, find, develop, and perfect our gifts, then we would have more control of our destiny.

It is our responsibility to find our gifts if we do not already know what they are. What you have inside you is valid. We all have different gifts, but one that I believe we all have, or can develop, but most often neglect, is the greatest gift of all—love. Love takes a lot of practice. It's easy to lose sight of love when there are so many things that cause anger, ego, pride, and other distractions. Along with developing talent, skill, or education, it is essential that you work on your heart.

Asking God for a clean heart is a good start. You'll be surprised how powerful prayer is, if you don't already know. Sometimes, I can't wait to be alone so that I can begin to reinvent myself and cleanse my heart. This is a self-developing job. Nobody can do this for you, because they can't reach inside you and hold your heart in their hands to make the necessary changes (unless, of course, it's your heart surgeon). You have to perform your own heart surgery. You should never have enough time on your hands to worry about other people—what they're doing or not doing, and why—when there's so much work that needs to be done on *you.* Instead of focusing on the one finger that you point at people, focus on the three fingers that are pointing back at you. Your job here on earth is to fix yourself. It's daily work, just like taking a shower. Pay attention to the way your heart beats. Go jogging. Cardiovascular exercises are good for your heart. Reaching your health and fitness goals, starts from the inside out. Seeking to lose, gain, or maintain your weight is pointless if you have a hateful, unhealthy heart. With proper, consistent training and development, the love muscle in your heart will keep growing to the point where there's no room in your heart for hate.

We all have skeletons in our closets, but many of us expect someone else to clean them out. Sometimes we leave them right in the closet, stinking! Just as it's your responsibility to clean your house before you sell it and buy a new one, it's also your responsibility to cleanse and restore your heart when you get home at night, before you begin a new day. I know it's easier said than done, but it's better done than said. We often take the easier route because it feels better, but the real power is in the healing, and the healing comes from dealing with the true matters in our hearts. Just as it is important to develop your voice for a good music career, it is as important to develop your heart for a good relationship. If you're looking for love, you should first make sure that love is what you have to offer.

Life can make us hard and tough. Past experiences or relationships teach us to be stronger and stand on our own so we don't get torn down or hurt again. We want to be independent because we don't want to put our lives in the hands of others and give them the power to crush us. Our society now forbids us to be weak. None of us wants to show our weak side, but it takes courage and trust to show weakness. Being strong is necessary sometimes; however, there is a time and place for everything. There's a time to be strong, but there's also a time to be soft, sensitive, caring, honest with our feelings, and weak. If we build a big brick wall around ourselves while we're looking for relationship, it could be a turnoff. The ones we're seeking relationship with may not want to fight with a wall in order to love us.

Being too "strong" all the time can cause an emotional blockage between you and someone special, and can sabotage what could be a good connection. I know, because I used to be guilty of this. Once I started giving myself the love I needed, I broke my own walls down. We have a way of trying to protect our hearts, and then become coldhearted, or heavy-hearted. But the heart was made to be soft! We need to reconstruct our hearts when we feel them crusting and hardening up, otherwise we're liable to give ourselves a heart attack. Everybody's so scared of love. Love is not the enemy. Hate is the enemy. Hate is what happens after you've been hurt, or had your share of experiences that make you shut down and change your heart from soft to hard. But the people that hurt you are the ones that need the love most. The love is what will rectify the problems—not hate. Hating others will only damage your own heart.

"Give me a clean heart." That's a song I sing, not necessarily to develop my vocals, but to develop my heart. Music is very therapeutic, and your voice is the best instrument. Always keep a song in your heart. Breathe deeply and use your voice as an instrument to heal yourself, instead of a weapon to destroy others—that's my focus. May your voice sound like music and be pleasing to the listening ear every time you use it.

CHAPTER 10

Rules of the Game

1. **You can't score if you don't take shots**. As an act, hobby, or task—or just to relieve tension—look at life as a game. Although that's not really true, have fun with it. Don't be scared to lose. How are you going to win if you don't play the game? Keep trying. Get up, get dressed, get out, and get on that court. Even if you haven't won yet, losing is still winning if you're learning. That's how you can keep your mind healthy, strong, and developed.

2. **No hating**. Hating is what sore losers do. I tell this to my very own kids when I see them doing it. If you hate the person that wins, you don't even deserve to play. Sit on the bench, watch, and learn. Don't hate the player or the game. All you need to do is change the way you play. Continue to search for different ways to train before you jump into the game. Find what works for you and be the best at it. There's always room to grow and improve. Loving yourself doesn't require hating someone else. Perfect your craft. You have your own purpose. If you know your purpose and are happy, there's no room or time for hate. Develop yourself, and be the best you can be.

3. **You have to lose the losers to win the winners.** Sometimes we block our own blessings by holding on to people, places, and things that don't serve us. Learn how to move forward gracefully. You will attract the right ones for your team. Losers aren't necessarily bad people. They just may not be the right ones for what you're trying

to do. Whether they're good people or not, if they're not strong components for your team, you're setting yourself up to lose. You can't make a cat bark, just as you can't make someone think like you, work as hard as you, or do the things you do the way you do them. Find someone who naturally has the mind-set you're looking for. When you make the right choices you'll start attracting the people you need for your life.

4. **Agree to disagree.** When someone disagrees with you, it doesn't mean that *you suck*. It only means that that person was given a mind of their own and that they see the situation from a different view. It's good to communicate and share views. Some of the things that make sense may stick with other people, and they'll change their views naturally on their own. If they don't, maybe they like their views better, and that's okay. Don't try to force anyone to agree with you. If everyone saw things the same way, there'd only be one recipe for making chicken. Life would be tasteless. If you disagree gracefully, you're agreeing to respect differences. Just move forward and enjoy each other's similarities.

5. **There are levels to the game.** If life had stairs, how high would you step up? It might be obvious for some that going all the way to the top is the objective, but other people get to the third step and stop. They may be comfortable with what they see on that level and want to live right there. Some people get tired and just want to take a break. You might find that bizarre if you had the vision to keep stepping up to the top. Some people plan on going to the top, but things happen and they change their minds and get scared of the unknown. So, fear makes them go back downstairs because they like the things behind them better and don't want to lose them. We are all people; we all bleed, breathe, and move our bowels. But we do not all think alike. Not everyone is on the same level. We have different mind-sets. As long as you are alive, there will always be stairs to climb. Whether or not to climb them is your choice. But if you understand that, then you shouldn't be so offended by others who have chosen to climb higher. If you're comfortable where you are, be happy. If you're not happy, learn from the ones who are on a higher level. Don't let insecurities stop you from looking up to

others who are deserving and worthy. I acknowledge and look up to people who are on higher levels then I am, the same way I would if I were a freshman in high school looking up to the seniors. After all, four years ago they were where I am now. Graduating is what I'm looking forward to. Some of us have a problem learning from our peers. But understand, some people do not like to stand in the same place, and everyone moves at a different pace. Others may be comfortable staying where they are. We are all different. There are levels to love relationships, the music business, and the game called life.

6. **Dress the part.** Dress for the things you want out of life, not for the *likes* and acceptance from everyone in your neighborhood—unless, of course, that's all you want out of life. If someone comes from another country to a city near you, will they be able to relate and feel comfortable with you? No matter where you go, be as strategic as you would if you were going to a job interview, business meeting, church, court, or anywhere else in the world. Dressing well says a lot, not only about the way you see yourself, but about the way you see others. Are they important enough for you to give them your best? They'll respect you more if you make them feel that they are. If you're single, ready to mingle and shack up, or even get married, then *man up and suit up,* or *dress up,* and beautify yourself. It's very attractive. It says a lot about your mentality and shows that you may be someone who makes wise decisions overall. A suit to a woman is like lingerie to a man. It's appealing! We become curious to see what's underneath. Can you imagine how a woman would feel if you dressed for her the way you would for a business meeting? Make her feel like a million bucks, then you can have whatever you like. And smelling good gains you extra points!

7. **Love it or leave it.** If you're dating or creating with someone, as time goes by, some things will turn you on, and other things will turn you off. Continue to build if you still need more clarity, but if you have gotten to the point where you know it won't work, don't hold on for your own selfish reasons. If you do hold on, let it be because you love the relationship and you're willing to learn more and do what it takes to make it work. If you know you don't feel

that way, just leave it alone. If you hold on to something you know you don't want, it can cause hateful feelings. When people come together because they honestly choose to *love it*, it's usually the best collaboration. If you don't *love it*, it's okay to *leave it* alone. You can't love and hate at the same time. That's trying to stand on two grounds. Choose the ground you want to stand on, and then stand strong. If you don't stand for something, you will fall for anything.

8. **Don't burn bridges.** We are all earth-mates. I believe we are all supposed to help each other out in one way or another. When you find that your time is up with someone, gracefully move on. That means moving forward with *respect*. You never know when the universe will have you crossing paths with someone again, but when it's time, make sure that path still exists. Pay attention to the things you say, and make sure the way you say them is constructive, not destructive. Being constructive in private keeps the bridges in place, so you can cross whenever time allows. But being destructive, especially in public, is lighting a fire. That's one sure way to burn a bridge.

9. **Love yourself.** You are and will always be the person you define yourself to be. If you believe you are beautiful, creative, talented, and special, then the truth is, you are—no matter what anyone else thinks. If you think you're not good enough, ugly, too fat, too skinny, too dark, useless, and hopeless, then others will think that about you too, because that's how you're coming across. If you accept yourself for who you are—flaws and all—then so will everyone else. And even if they don't, that's their problem, not yours. Don't be concerned with the way other people see you, unless it's someone you trust and they're sincerely being honest and constructive. Otherwise, that is one of the worst pressures we can put on ourselves. There's nothing wrong with honesty when you know you need improvement. Surround yourself with others who are honest if you genuinely like to improve yourself. Love yourself enough to want to make improvements. Other people can't help what they see, and it is human nature to be judgmental. If someone tells you that you've gained weight or have bad breath, it may not be a bad idea to check yourself and see if it's true. It may not be any

of their business, and maybe they could have found a more tactful way of saying it, but if their eyes see the weight gain or their nose smells the bad breath, are they wrong for being honest? If you have a problem with someone being honest, then start being more honest with yourself. When someone tells me I've gained weight, I say, "Yeah, I know!" How can I be mad at them for seeing the truth? Yes, beware of insecure people that tell you the truth and alter it just to bring you down, but if you love yourself enough you can tell whether someone is being constructive or destructive. You can feel when someone is trying to pick you up and help you or knock you down and hurt you because they've been hurt. Hurt people *hurt people!* Love yourself enough to accept constructive criticism from those who love you and wish to see you grow. But love yourself enough to remove yourself when you can see that others are being destructive and judgmental.

10. **God first**. I'm not too involved in religion, but I'm very spiritual. My life is less complicated and confusing, and more structured and purposeful, when I pray and put God first. It's human nature to have a variety of emotions. Feelings change like the weather. Many of us make major decisions based on temporary feelings, and then when the feelings come down we try to undo things that may not be undoable. Before you act, allow yourself to feel. Give yourself ample time to let your feelings reach their peak and come down, and then think about the best thing to do before you move. Consult God before you act. We all have our own emotions and reasoning's but spiritually speaking, "lean not unto your own understanding." Realize that beyond your emotions and logic there is a spiritual purpose much bigger than your own way. You are on this earth for a reason. Before you pick up the phone and call friends and family, get on your knees and ask God. Friends, family, husbands, wives, kids, teachers, or anyone in human flesh may not have all of the answers you are looking for. The best business about any business is handling your own business. Make it your business to search for the truth about yourself. First, find God. Then, find yourself. *Then,* you'll find the right people for your team, whether the dream is to find love, make music, or simply *win* in this game called life.

Printed in the United States
By Bookmasters